Secrets of the Top Equestrian Trainers

Secrets of the Top Equestrian Trainers

Interviews with
TINA SEDERHOLM

D&C

David and Charles

A DAVID & CHARLES BOOK

David & Charles is a subsidiary of F+W (UK) Ltd.,
an F+W Publications Inc. company

First published in the UK in 2005

Photographs by Kit Houghton except the following:
David & Charles/Matthew Roberts: endpapers, opposite p1, p2, p6
Mark Rashid: p123

Distributed in North America
by F&W Publications, Inc.
4700 East Galbraith Road
Cincinnati, OH 45236
1-800-289-0963

A catalogue record for this book is available from the British Library.

ISBN 0 7153 2152 8

Printed in Malta by Gutenberg Press Ltd
for David & Charles
Brunel House   Newton Abbot   Devon

Commissioning Editor: Jane Trollope
Art Editor: Sue Cleave
Layout: Jodie Lystor
Desk Editor: Louise Crathorne
Project Editor: Anne Plume

Visit our website at www.davidandcharles.co.uk

David & Charles books are available from all good bookshops;
alternatively you can contact our Orderline on (0)1626 334555 or write to
us at FREEPOST EX2110, David & Charles Direct, Newton Abbot, TQ12 4ZZ
(no stamp required UK mainland).

Contents

Introduction	6
Goran 'Yogi' Breisner, the Coach's Coach	9
Peter Charles and the Business of Show Jumping	25
Richard Davison: Take Your Own Line	39
Robert Dover and the Path to Excellence	53
Henrietta Knight: Stay True to What You Believe In	65
Anne Kursinski: Keeping It Simple	77
Kyra Kyrklund: Working with What You've Got	91
David O'Connor and the Language of Horses	101
Rodrigo Pessoa: Focus, Focus, Focus	113
Mark Rashid and the Art of Passive Leadership	123
Afterword	135
Index	136

Introduction

If you were given the chance to ask your equestrian heroes anything you wanted, what questions would you pose? More to the point, who would you choose? These were the challenges I was faced with, when I was asked to write this book. After discussing it with friends, and looking back over the schools of thought that have influenced me, I decided on this particular group of riders and trainers. They come from a variety of equestrian spheres: dressage, eventing, racing, show jumping and natural horsemanship. I have known several of them since I was very young, others I have studied from a distance, and a couple of them are recent acquaintances.

Some, such as Rodrigo Pessoa and David O'Connor, have achieved spectacular competitive results, winning Olympic medals, World Championships and World Cups. Others, such as Yogi Breisner and Anne Kursinski, have trained multitudes of stylish and successful riders. They have all produced winning horses, in particular Peter Charles and Henrietta Knight. Each of them has made great inroads into understanding the psychology of horses, and each has had a significant influence on the sport they are involved in.

But results are simply that, results: a culmination of work, attention, dedication, successes and failures; so I decided to find out what was at the core of their success. In the same way as when I am learning Pilates the success of every exercise depends on me engaging my deep stomach muscles and pelvic floor, I wanted to identify the roots that support these trainers' methods. Then, I felt, I would have discovered the magic behind it all.

I hope this book will inspire, educate and entertain you. I hope it will make you think a little deeper about how to build better relationships with your horses, and the hows and whys of good results, whatever your field of endeavour might be.

It is impossible to make a definitive list of the best riders and trainers in the world, and anyway, how would you ever begin to measure that? However, these ten have inspired me greatly over the years, whether that was watching them in the ring, giving a clinic, or working with them at home. They are thought-provoking, intelligent, and sometimes contentious. I hope you enjoy reading their words as much as I did listening to them.

Note: Much of the material in this book comes from conversations that I had with these riders and trainers. In order to give the reader a strong sense of each individual, much of the text is directly quoted from those conversations, and for ease of understanding, my words are in italics.

Goran 'Yogi' Breisner, the Coach's Coach

Yogi Breisner

Yogi is one of the most versatile trainers in Great Britain, and has had a profound influence in both horse trials and the racing world. Formerly an international three-day event himself, he has been World Class Performance Manager to the British three-day event team for the past five years, and is a consultant to the British Racing School. Well known for his unflappable temperament, he is also a most generous trainer, who always has time for any rider, of any level, who is having a problem.

Driving down the road of comfortable yet unobtrusive houses where Yogi lives, it strikes me that you would never imagine that this was home to one of the most influential people in modern three-day eventing. But as Yogi welcomes me into his house, looking relaxed and with his customary packet of cigars in his hand, I remember how large this house is, and how thoughtfully equipped. I also remember how much time he spent extending and modernizing it, and I realize this is wholly indicative of the man himself.

I first met Yogi when he came to my father's training centre, Waterstock, in Oxfordshire, in 1978. I was ten years old, and he had just had his first attempt at Badminton. We used to joke around with him a lot, especially because of his accent, a mixture of the guttural tones typical of his native Skåne, Sweden, which had been exacerbated by more than three years spent in Ireland, where he had picked up the strong inflections of the County Meath accent. Yogi took it all in his stride, with a wry smile on his face. It seems he always does.

Yogi spent thirteen years at Waterstock, and during that time he became a respected competitor on the international horse trials scene. He was regularly placed in the top ten at Badminton and Burghley, and twice had the distinction of recording the fastest time cross-country at Badminton. He was also a member of the gold medal-winning Swedish team at the European Championships in Frauenfeld, and a member of the Swedish Olympic team in Los Angeles. His most successful horse was Ultimus, a wiry ex-racehorse bought off the racetrack in Sweden. Hampered by poor movement in the trot, which usually left him trailing a few marks after the dressage, he was nevertheless a jumping machine, and would gallop cross-country in such a fluid way it was as if the fences just dissolved underneath him.

Yogi retired from competitive riding in 1987, but continued in his role as my father's right-hand man at Waterstock, teaching extensively and managing the day-to-day running of the training centre. In 1991, though, it was time for a change, and he struck out as a freelance instructor – although he could often still be found at Waterstock working with the racehorses that had come in for reschooling.

There had always been a smattering of racehorses at Waterstock, usually those that had fallen whilst racing and lost either their confidence or their technique, or those that were difficult to manoeuvre around a racecourse. But this was a sphere that Yogi began to make his own, and in addition to travelling the country giving clinics and teaching riders of all levels, he was in demand with the leading National Hunt trainers, working with such big winners as Master Oats and Alderbrook.

It was, in fact, as if things had turned a full circle. When he first bought Ultimus from the racetrack in Täby, it was because he had been an amateur jockey who wanted to ride in National Hunt races in Sweden. It was only when Ultimus showed such aptitude for show jumping, and later cross-country when hunting with the Co. Meath and Tara hounds, that Yogi decided to take him eventing.

After several years, having been crowned a jumping 'guru' in National Hunt circles, Yogi was approached to become World Class Performance Manager to the British event team. This was in 1999, just eight months before the Sydney Olympics. At this point the team results at the last couple of Olympic Games had been rather disappointing, yet we had some of the finest riders in the world. Armed with that knowledge, how was Yogi going to make a difference, especially in such a short amount of time?

Creating the right atmosphere

'First I looked at what had gone wrong in the past, because I came on the back of some fairly mediocre results from the British team. Also I had to look at what material we had available, and then what I could contribute.

'What became quite obvious was that when these riders went by themselves to Badminton or Burghley, they performed. Put them in a team, and they didn't. My feeling was that I needed to create an environment in which they could work as if they were on their own.

'I remember that at the same time as I got this job, the English football team had done badly at the European Championships. When the players and their manager, Kevin Keegan, had been interviewed, they all emphasized what a great atmosphere there had been in the team. There had been nothing wrong with that. I thought to myself, it just shows you can have a good atmosphere without it being the right one.

'That is what I made important. To have the right atmosphere, where the competitors feel comfortable to perform at their best. I once listened to a talk by the Olympic swimmer Adrian Moorhouse, and he said that on the wall at the pool where he trained was a sign that read, "We want to create an atmosphere where excellence will prevail." That is what I strive for.'

TINA: *The difference between 'good' and 'right' resonated with me. I know when I was competing, there were days when I knew I was going to do well. There was a certain calmness and solidity I felt inside. However, especially at the beginning of my career this was a bit of a hit-and-miss affair, and so I wondered how Yogi created the 'right' atmosphere at the appropriate moment.*

Reviewing and planning

'I do a lot of self-examination. One of the benefits of being a freelance instructor is that I might do a couple of hours' work in one place, and then jump in the car to get to the next place. This gives me plenty of thinking time to plan for the next client. In this way I prepare for a coaching session, and then review it afterwards.

'I take a similar attitude with the team. Every evening, just before I fall asleep, I revisit the whole day to analyse the instructions I have given to people. Were they right or wrong? How were they received? Is there anyone I haven't spoken to enough?

'Then on the basis of these thoughts, I would plan how I would approach the next day, both generally and with individual people. So, for instance, if one day the whole team was extremely jolly, and there was a lot of banter and laughter and jokes flying about, I would say to myself that is great, because it means there is a wonderful spirit in the camp. But you can't do that all the time because it goes overboard, so maybe tomorrow I would have a bit of a sterner expression on my face, be a little quieter, stronger rather than humorous with my comments. On the other hand, if the riders had been very serious, I might come out more lighthearted.'

TINA: *As Yogi pointed out, part of the problem was that whilst British riders were outstanding individually, when they were put in a team they under-performed. How did he overcome this problem?*

The individual approach

'What's important to remember is that we are all individuals, so what is right for one person is not always right for another. William (Fox-Pitt), for instance, thrives on watching other people and asking them questions. On the other hand, once Pippa (Funnell) has walked a course for the last time and

'In a team sport like football, everyone has to know each other inside out, so they can pre-guess what another team member is going to do. In equestrian sports, if each individual does their best you will win a gold medal.'

made her final preparations, she will not think about the course again between that time and when she goes into the ten-minute box. She does not want to be distracted by the opinions of others.

'In a team sport like football or rowing, everyone has to work together and know each other inside out, so they can pre-guess what another team member is going to do. You don't need this in equestrian sports, because if each individual does their best you will win a gold medal. So it is not necessary to build team spirit in the same way.

'Of course, occasionally a rider might have to forgo individual medal aspirations for the sake of the team, perhaps by taking a longer route at a chancy fence in order to play safe, but risk incurring a few time penalties. Then it is helpful if the team is close-knit because they can support each other. But this is a pretty rare situation.'

TINA: *Although the theory behind the job of keeping this atmosphere balanced and effective is a simple and sound one, it is rarely an easy job. It takes moment-to-moment assessment of the situation, and the need to be flexible enough to be able to change course instantly if necessary.*

In Sydney, the team was lying in silver medal position after the cross-country phase, but had lost their experienced anchorman, Ian Stark, to a fall in the water. Of the three remaining riders, only one of them had been on a championship team once before.

Going for silver

'When I went to bed on the night after the cross-country in Sydney I did my normal analysis of the day. We were one and a half fences behind the Australians, and we seriously had the better show jumpers. I felt, for right or wrong, that our biggest enemy for my 'novice' riders was that they would feel that they could win gold, and would try too hard.

'Once the horses had passed the vetting, I sat them all down in the tackroom, and said, "Look, we are not going to win gold. The Aussies have led the whole way through. If you go out and try to win gold, you will only get disappointed when you win silver (they had a lot of fences in hand over the third-placed American team). Let's just go out there and jump. Just make sure you don't go the wrong way, and jump as if you were at home, and let's enjoy winning silver."

'I thought if I could get them to do that, then they wouldn't try too hard and that would win us the gold.

'They all turned around and said, "That's not like you, Yogi. We know you want to win that gold medal as much as we do, and we are bloody well going to win that medal," and out they stormed.

'I sat in the tackroom, and thought, I've failed. And I was right. They tried so hard that they had fences down, and we ended up in silver medal position.'

TINA: *After Sydney, Yogi took the show-jumping weakness seriously, and a lot of concentrated work went into improving it over the winter. He and Kenneth Clawson (team show-jumping trainer) held several training sessions, and brought over Albert Voorn, who had just won an individual silver medal in the show jumping in Sydney, to train longlisted riders. They worked principally on improving the quality of the horses' show-jumping canter, and on riding courses in such a way that they would not get time penalties.*

The result was that in the Europeans the following year in Pau, their strong show-jumping performances maintained their gold medal position, and in the World Championships in Jerez, the British actually won their medals because of their good show-jumping performance. In Athens, they managed to pull even more of a miracle out of the bag, when they dropped from bronze to fourth position overnight due to an injury to William Fox-Pitt's Tamarillo.

Sticking to a system

'Cross-country finished at mid-day in Athens, and the riders went down to relax at the beach. I stayed behind because there was a problem with William's horse. Although the vet had not given up hope, I knew in the bottom of my heart that the horse was not going to be sound enough to show jump, so I got the results sheet out and started calculating the scores. When the riders came back, we trotted the horses up and made the decision not to present Tamarillo at the vets' inspection. Obviously William was very downhearted and was on his way back to the stables with the horse. Being a very close team, they wanted to go with him, but I held them back for a few moments. I told them, "Look, we have been through a lot together. I have had a look at the scores and we have a real chance of winning a medal. But tomorrow we are just going to stick to our usual system of warming up, and are just going to go in there and jump."

'I told them the one thing I was not going to do was keep score. I didn't want to know which rider's score was going to make the difference. I told them, "It is out of our hands. We cannot control what the other three teams will do. We can only control what we do. So we are going to concentrate on jumping to the best of our ability and what will be, will be."

'And that's what we did. When Pippa, who was the last Brit to go, jumped her round, Tracie Robinson (dressage trainer to the team) came out and told me, if the American had one down, we would get bronze. If the French had two down, we would get silver. If the German had three down, we would win the gold.

'So then the American went in, and had one down. The French went in and had one down, and then Bettina went in and jumped, but I did not see that because we were so busy celebrating. We had won a bronze out of absolutely nothing. As we were hugging each other, absolutely jubilant, Nick Skelton came down and asked me if I had seen Bettina's round. I said no, and he told me, she went over the start line twice. She should have a stop and time penalties. He said "I've watched a bit of show jumping in my life and there is no way that was a clear round." So I went to the Ground Jury to find out what was happening, but the French and Americans had beaten me to it!'

TINA: *The rest, as they say, is history, with Great Britain eventually promoted to silver medal position. Yogi's approach in this situation reminded me of a book called* Mental Toughness Training for Sports: *when talking about the wrong attitude towards winning, it cited 'winning is everything' as one of the most self-defeating attitudes a sportsman could have. However, in a note at the bottom of the page it read:*

'...Winning is, in fact, everything!' This realization, however, does not change the fact that as athletes become preoccupied or obsessed with winning, performances will show a steady deterioration in the majority of cases. Performance consequences are considerably better when you focus on performing your best and then proceed to establish and carefully maintain the right internal conditions, rather than focusing on winning.

However, even the best laid plans still have an element of risk or chance in them. If the British team made up ground in the show jumping, it was because they had to, having made mistakes, albeit minor ones, in the cross-country in both Jerez and Athens.

Making use of mistakes

'I think that in Jerez we lost it through three things. Bad decisions, that in my opinion were not bad decisions at the time, but in retrospect turned out that way. We were the first team that was in contention out on the course, and there was one fence that was a bit chancy. We decided to go the short route with the two last team horses in order to ensure gold. And they both had a stop. We lost team gold, and possibly individual gold and silver, and had we won those, we would have looked like heroes. But we made the decision that rather than play conservative and win silver, we would go for gold. In retrospect, if we had played safe, and gone clear we still might have won gold. But we all have twenty-twenty vision in hindsight!

'Secondly, the mistakes that gave us those two stops were, in my opinion, 50 per cent bad luck, and 50 per cent horse-and-rider error. Now after this, there are people who would go on a lot about those mistakes, and say you must tell the riders where they went wrong and put a lot of pressure on. I actually come from the other angle because I know that the riders *know* where they went wrong, and I don't want to rub salt in those wounds. And I would never criticise them outside the team structure, especially to the press. This is because I believe long term that public criticism could affect them badly.

'I think there is no point raking over the coals afterwards, but I would certainly log those mistakes in my mind and make use of them in the future. For instance, if we came to a similar fence on a course, I would say to the rider, look, just go a little steadier than you did in Jerez into this one.

'When we sat having dinner on the evening of the cross-country in Jerez, after we had dropped from gold to fourth place and were out of the individual placings, I asked them if they wanted to discuss this, as we had obviously made the wrong decision. The consensus from the team was this: we have created a positive team that is going to championships to win gold. Some of the team members had been on teams when the main aim was to complete, but now they felt they had gone beyond that mentality. They felt we had made the right decision.'

TINA: *As John F. Kennedy said, 'In order to succeed greatly, you have to risk failing greatly.' No one is going to win all the time, and the margins in modern three-day eventing are so narrow, it is often a little bit of luck that tips the balance.*

There is no doubt that Yogi puts his whole self into producing excellent team results and keeping his riders on track mentally. His demeanour is one of quiet enthusiasm,

'There are people who say you must tell the riders where they went wrong and put a lot of pressure on. I actually come from the other angle because I know that the riders *know* where they went wrong.'

and if you see him at a competition, it will almost certainly be by the ringside, perhaps smoking a cigar, unobtrusively observing the riders. He might have a few words with one of them, but if you did not know him, you could be forgiven for thinking he was just another spectator. This almost certainly helps the riders to be more at their ease, but how does Yogi create this state of mind in himself?

Finding an outlet

'When you are in a team environment, and you go to a high-pressure com-petition, not only do you have that pressure, but there are chef d'equipe meetings, vets, other trainers, owners and support staff to deal with, plus the media and interviews. In that situation I am bombarded with things from 6.30 a.m. until 9 o'clock at night for as much as a week continuously.

'You are only human, and if you are going to have a calm front in that situa-tion, you need to have something to help your brain let go. Personally I always need space, and some time on my own. In fact I would say that the main reason for me jogging is not so much to keep myself fit, but to keep my brain right. If you compete, your adrenalin runs high, but you get to release it through the effort of riding. Standing on the sidelines, I get just as pent up as the riders do, but I don't get that adrenalin release, or the calmness that follows. Instead I might go for a run or watch some rubbish on TV, to find that relaxation.'

TINA: *What surprised, and also heartened me, is that despite his calm exterior, Yogi also gets very nervous.*

Overcoming nerves

'I think a lot of good coaches have this in common. To the outside, they look very confident, sure of themselves, almost to the point of being arrogant.

In addition to being employed by UK Sport as World Class Performance Manager, Yogi is also employed by British Eventing as national coach. This role sees him in charge of the overall education of event riders in this country, both the ones of international standard, as well as organizing the regional and grass roots' training programme.

He is also instrumental in moves to raise the standard of coaching and instruction in this country, and is particularly interested in the way knowledge and teaching material can be presented more effectively. One way he does this is to use the acronym 'CLOCK' to demonstrate his basic philosophy behind successful coaching.

C stands for communication.

Unless a trainer explains simply and clearly what, and why, they are doing something, the rider is unlikely to be able to carry out their demands.

L stands for listening.

Both with the ears to what the rider has to say, and, as Yogi puts it, also 'with the eyes'. By this he means that a good coach observes the horse and rider closely, so he/she can make an accurate assessment of the current situation, and pick up on what most needs to be improved.

O is for organized.

As far as Yogi is concerned, you need to have a good plan for the lesson, and to conduct yourself in an organized fashion if you are going to be an effective and respected coach.

C stands for confidence.

The good coach is confident in what they are doing, and inspires confidence in their pupils, so creating an atmosphere that is conducive to learning.

K is for keep it simple.

When explanations and exercises are as simple as possible, there is much more chance that your pupils will understand you.

Finally the word 'CLOCK' also reminds coaches to make the effort to run to time as much as possible.

But underneath they are insecure, and I would certainly say that beneath it all, I am very insecure. The uncertainty I feel, walking round an Olympic track with someone like William or Leslie, is almost to the point of being petrified, thinking I must get this right.

'I think this is true of a lot of people who perform well. Jamie Osborne, who was one of the finest jump jockeys of the eighties and nineties, told me that before most races he was so unsure of himself that the only way that he could hide that from the owner or the trainer was to crack jokes. Even a person like Bjorn Borg sometimes had to physically force himself to get off the chair in between games in his tennis matches.

'But this insecurity focuses me, and makes me really plan well, and that gives me the security I am lacking. So for instance, in order to do a good job with the team riders, I would have walked the course beforehand and spent a lot of time thinking about what advice to give each particular person, in advance of walking the course with the team.'

Creating confidence

'I think confidence is very nearly the be-all and end-all. I have seen so many examples of someone who is confident, and yet doing things wrong, who wins over someone who is much better, but is lacking confidence. As an instructor, I consciously work a lot on confidence. Creating confidence is closely related to the way you communicate and build up trust, whether that is with another person, or with a horse. This revolves around reading the signals you are given and reacting in the right way, whether this is with a rider you are training, or when you are walking into a young horse's stable to put a bridle on for the first time.

'You need to watch their body language, and see, where do I need to go a little stronger, where do I back off? Make no mistake about it, I have got this wrong a million times and there are times I have shouted and screamed far too much.

'As you grow older though, you realize that this behaviour does not really work, because apart from anything else, if you have shouted and been sarcastic with someone, you still haven't got a result and you walk away feeling bad inside. But if you are nice about it and have tried your hardest to figure it out, and it still has not worked, at least you don't walk away with that sick feeling in your stomach.

'There was a famous trotting trainer in Sweden in the sixties called Sören Nordin. He wrote that if you need to discipline a horse, you must never do it when you are upset or angry, or when your own heart rate is running high. Your body temperature, your heart rate and your mental state should be as if you were sitting in an armchair at home. Then if you give them a telling-off, it penetrates. But if you do it when you are emotionally high, it upsets the horse, and he does not register the punishment, he only gets upset about it. If you do it from total calmness, he will take it, but not get worried or shy afterwards. With age, I think I am making more and more use of that advice, with both horses and human beings.'

> **TINA:** *Another of Yogi's simple rules that he uses in order to keep up the quality of his work is to refrain from using the word 'Don't'. How often do you hear 'Don't look down!' yelled across an arena? And yet it is almost impossible to not do something. Instead, Yogi would replace that statement with something like 'Look where you are going!', which has a twofold effect: it directly informs the rider of what they need to do, and it saves unnecessary criticism.*

Recognize the core problem

'One of the most important things in any form of coaching is to remember that we are here to develop talent, not destroy it. A coach has to learn to use their judgement. For instance, a rider might be doing something that is technically incorrect, but which does not affect their overall performance. Yet the same fault in another rider might be damaging to their riding, and would need to be corrected.

'It is important as a coach to recognize what is relevant to change, and what is not. You don't want to take away from someone's personal make-up and character. Moreover, when you are assessing a rider you want to find out where

expert insight

'When you are assessing a rider you want to find out where the core problem lies. For example, you might be watching someone who has terrible hands. But when you look closely, you see that the core issue is not their hands, but their lack of balance.'

the core problem lies. For example, you might be watching someone who has terrible hands. But when you look closely, you see that the core issue is not their hands, but their lack of balance, which is causing them to grab hold of the horse's mouth. Therefore the lack of balance is what needs to be addressed, and when that is improved, the hands will settle automatically.'

TINA: *When Yogi first starts to work with a horse and rider, whether that is for the first time, or with one he might not have seen for a while, he allows himself a few moments to watch the horse and rider working. He looks at the overall impression he gets from them, paying particular attention to how they are mentally. Are they confident or unsure? Do they look like they trust each other? Of course this mental picture is given away by the physicality both horse and rider demonstrate. For instance, if a rider tightens the hand and tells the horse off at the slightest spook, this lets Yogi know that they are a bit unsure of the horse.*

He will then talk to the rider about what they want to achieve, and what they feel are their challenges with the horse. From this he can build up a picture of what they are like, and what the best starting point for their improvement will be.

Now with many years of coaching behind him, Yogi is holding a big vision for the future of horse trials; in his own words:

An operational training plan

'If I could leave a legacy in British Eventing, it would be that there was a proper structure to the training within the various teams. This has already started in small ways, but I want to develop it more, as well as developing coaching techniques.

'I would like to get a more effective, streamlined team management. All four teams – ponies, Juniors, Young Riders and Seniors – need a proper operational plan. The Senior one is already in action, but the other three teams need to be updated. If we have a proper operational plan, it will show us to be a truly professional sport to any potential funding body, as well as defining a specific route for potential team riders.

'I want this plan to identify young riders with future team potential, and educate them in two ways. Firstly, that there is an education programme that ensures that by the time a rider gets to Senior level, their education is done. And I don't mean just about riding: it is also about looking after their horses in the right way, getting them fit, keeping them sound, and so on. The other strand would be the training that happens specifically to prepare teams for championships.'

TINA: *This creation of a more direct and obvious route to develop young talent links in with the aims of UK Sport for athletes across the board: in short, a structured approach that produces more professional athletes.*

A long-term development programme

'At the moment the system is that the World Class Potential Squads get together for a couple of days' training with a top class coach, where I am sure they learn a lot. But there is no follow-up to that work, and that is what I want to introduce. I want us to look into what the riders are doing well, and where there are gaps in their knowledge, say a shortcoming in their seat, or the condition of their horse. Then they would be given targets in the areas that they need to improve.

'After six weeks, I want to get them all back together again, and see what improvement has been made in their particular area, so they can be given new targets, either in the same or a new area.'

expert insight

'If you look at the evolution of cross-country courses, where narrow fences are now put together on related distances, you have come back to forward riding, because related distances demand that.'

TINA: *What this will produce, instead of isolated islands of good quality training, is the possibility for steady and solid progression. However, a long-term development programme such as this may seem a far cry from the days when British riders were made in the hunting field, and if you had one good horse, you had a fighting chance of getting to Badminton or even the Olympic Games, the way it still was when Yogi competed at top level.*

Encouraging forward riding

'My view is that no one can stop evolution, whether it is good or bad. You can steer it in certain areas, but you cannot stop it, and therefore you have to live with it and take what is there. For instance, it is often commented that as cross-country courses have become more technical with a lot of turns and arrowheads, it has made the competitors ride backwards, whereas if you have big straightforward fences it makes them ride forwards. However, if you look at the evolution of cross-country courses, where narrow fences are now put together on related distances, you have come back to the forward riding, because related distances demand that.'

TINA: *Yogi also pointed out that although courses are more technical than perhaps ten years ago, the basic training for them remains the same.*

Training the basics

'Of course, we train at home over narrow points, and jumping single barrels and so on, but to me the more important thing to train to enable the horse and rider to cope with the technical fences is the basics. It is the rider's ability on the flat to ride the horse straight, to get the horse into the outside hand, to ride turns well and straighten up afterwards. It is as simple as making sure that if you intend to jump the fence in the middle that you actually do that, and also making sure you are straight before and after the fence.

'If you do that basic work right, then narrow fences are not an issue, you only need to train over them for familiarity's sake, just as you would introduce a young horse to coloured fillers or water trays.'

TINA: *It is reassuring to hear that someone who holds a vision for event riders becoming modern professional athletes also has his roots firmly in solid traditional training. What Yogi reminded me is that there are no magical shortcuts, or if there is magic to be had, it is in sound, genuine training for the horses and riders, and helping the riders maintain a mental state where they can bring out the best in themselves.*

Putting the pieces in the right place

'Success is not one big thing, because if it were, it would be very easy to achieve. To me, it is a combination of an awful lot of small things. Like a puzzle, you need to put all the little pieces together, and the one who gets the pieces in the right place, they are the ones who succeed.'

Peter Charles and the Business of Show Jumping

Peter Charles

The linchpin of the Irish show-jumping team for more than 20 years, Peter is one of the most experienced show jumpers in the world. A former European Champion, and three times winner of the Hickstead Derby, he combines a sharp business sense with being a stylish and effective rider, and having an excellent eye for a horse. A strong advocate of correct training methods, he has an infectious enthusiasm for the game of show jumping, and approaches the production and training of horses with a strong dose of common sense.

I am not the first in the queue on the day that I go to visit Peter. A lady is waiting on the front doorstep, and with a note of panic in her voice says, 'Can I see him first?'. So I wander down to the stable yard, past the garden where there is a set of toy show jumps, mirrored by a somewhat larger and more complicated course in the outdoor arena.

Eventually I meet up with him. Inside the recently renovated farmhouse, where the walls are covered alternately with photographs of Peter competing and his children's latest artwork, we sit down with a couple of mugs of tea and a plate of chocolate biscuits.

Peter has won competitions all over the world. Brought up in England, but receiving most of his show-jumping education in Ireland, Peter switched nationality in 1992, and has been a member of the Irish team for nearly every major championship and Nations Cup since then, the high point being his victory in the European Championships at St Gallen in1995.

His major victories also include the Grand Prix in Calgary, the Hickstead Derby three times in a row, as well as having won in excess of ten cars. More than this, he has made a profitable business out of horses and show jumping, something many people find almost impossible to do.

Top class horses for top class riders

'Every penny I've I earned, I've earned out of horses. I've bought and sold them, and I've always risked more money than I've been able to afford, buying horses. I've bought horses that I've known I am going to have to find the money for from somewhere, and I've walked away thinking "How the hell am I going to pay for that?" But I can't turn a good horse down if I see it. I have to buy it. I've never left one behind yet that I wanted to buy, whether I've got the money or not. I found the money, or borrowed the money…I'd have even mortgaged my house if I'd seen the right one – not that I ever got to that stage, and I wouldn't need to now – but that's how strongly I feel.

'It's like anything, if you try and buy really good horses, they are a lot easier to sell than bad ones. I'd rather pay ten or twenty thousand pounds more for the horse that I want, than compromise and buy something lesser for cheaper. Because if you have a product that somebody wants – and the market is now so select and fragile in the amount of good horses that are coming through – you've got several buyers for that horse, so your profit will be greater.

'Also, it's so much easier to live every day with a talented horse than with

> 'It's like anything, if you try and buy really good horses, they are a lot easier to sell than bad ones. I'd rather pay ten or twenty thousand pounds more for the horse that I want, than compromise and buy something lesser for cheaper.'

a second-rate one, unless you are buying for a specific market. I try to buy for mainly top class riders. As for myself, I generally sell everything, unless an owner has bought one and he wants to keep it. I do like to buy and sell. I've bought and sold property, advised people on buying big properties, and put together syndicates to buy certain horses.'

TINA: *Because Peter is as courageous when selling his horses as he is when buying them, he is ensured a steady through-flow of talented horses to compete on.*

Selling to the right person

'I've never been afraid of selling. Horses are always being bred, so there is always another in the pipeline. It is getting harder to find them, but because I am involved with the business I have a greater tendency to come across good horses than most people do. It has got harder now because people are either not selling, or you are up against some very rich private individuals. But you should never be afraid to pay a good price for a horse.

'I don't always look at a horse with me in mind, and I believe a lot of riders make that mistake. They look at a horse and ask themselves, is it a superstar for *them*. I look at the horse and say, "Who would this horse suit?" I really look at it in this light: "Who would buy this horse? Which rider?" I try to imagine where this horse will end up in life. Is he a 1.40m horse, a Young Rider's horse? Might he make an eventer even? That's the way I go about it. If he knocks my socks off, that's a bonus.

'I'm very fussy. I love a horse with a perfect technique, I really love it when the front end just disappears, the back end cracks out behind, and he really rounds over his fences, scopey and nice to ride. That's the dream horse.

'I don't have my sights set in stone though, and they don't have to fit that bill. But their ambition has to be always to try and leave the fences up to some degree. If they make a mistake and knock it down, they don't have to be perfect and give it two feet, but they must have a conscience. They also need to have a good brain to work out how to get from A to B. If it's a young horse, I look to see if they can they work out their striding easily, and how well balanced they are. If he's a big horse, he may be more on his forehand, but training and time will improve the balance no end.'

> **TINA:** *Peter does hold the record for the number of phone calls (five) taken during an interview. At least two are about horses he is due to see that afternoon; one of them has called to say that as it is raining perhaps Peter better not come. As he puts the phone down, Peter smiles and comments that this is the second time that rider, who does not own the horse, has tried to put him off, so he thinks he definitely better go now. However, despite this voracious appetite for buying and selling and competing horses, Peter did not come into show jumping in an auspicious way, or at a particularly early age.*

Inauspicious beginnings

'I became a rider because I was a failed football player. I was born in Bootle, in Liverpool, very close to Anfield. I loved football, watched football, tried like hell to play football. My sister and my mother had a love of horses and I would tag along behind my sister when she went to ride at a place outside Liverpool, and ride a bit myself.

'I can genuinely say that I got into horses because my parents died. It's a sad truth, but had they lived I most probably would never have been allowed to get into horses to the level I did. I'd've been made to go to school and finish my education. Instead I left school when I was fifteen and went to Ireland with the sole ambition of trying to follow my dream.

expert insight

'I love a horse with a perfect technique, I really love it when the front end just disappears, the back end cracks out behind, and he really rounds over his fences, scopey and nice to ride. That's the dream horse.'

'I started quite late compared to all the other kids. My career wasn't planned from an early age, and all that nonsense. I fell into it. If I could have been a footballer, I'd've done that because it was my first love, and I still love and actively follow football. I love the technique and management side of it, watching how they get new players. It's not unlike show jumping in a way, managing a team of show jumpers. Trying to develop young horses through is pretty much the same as trying to spot talent and bring it on in any sport.'

TINA: *Soon after arriving in Ireland, Peter went to Iris Kellet's, at that time the most famous riding school in the country. It was a tough time for him because, not being one of the paying clients, Peter worked in return for his lessons, and worked very hard indeed.*

Iris Kellet and Eddie Macken

'It was seriously hard physical work at Iris Kellet's, for one lesson a week. But she spurred me on because she told me I wasn't any good. It didn't do me any harm at the time, but had I been able to put all that energy into riding and training, I'd've come along a lot quicker. That situation improved when I started to ride a few more horses, and after a couple of years I left there looking quite respectable. I was able to ride in a nice position. One thing she was really good at, was that she always bashed into you the basic fundamentals of how to sit and how to ride properly on the flat. That was always her motto, to stay in balance with your horse.

'Then I was fortunate enough to be offered a job with Eddie Macken. Ned Cash (a legendary Irish horse dealer), said to Eddie "Eh, he can ride a bit, that lad, you want to get him," so Eddie offered me a job.

'I remember going there, I had a Honda 50 that was made up of bits I borrowed off other peoples' bikes at the time, no insurance, no licence or anything. I stuck all my gear on the back of it, tied on with baling string, and it broke down about five miles out and I had to push it the rest of the way.

'When I went to work for Eddie Macken, he was the number one rider in Ireland by a long way. He had what I would call true superstar status, and that went beyond show jumping. Eddie was in all the main magazines, in TV commercials, and he had a great sponsorship. It was a global sport then, and a focal point in Ireland, on the TV every night. You could see the demands on his time, how he coped in life, he just breezed through. He had a good way of just bouncing into shows and getting on with it. I looked at how he did it and why he did it, and it was the sort of education money couldn't buy.

'We argued quite a bit over different things. The more I progressed, the more I felt I could do things better, until one day he said, "The only way you'll find out, lad, is by getting out there and doing it." So I said, "Right, I will!"'

TINA: *After leaving Eddie's, Peter had two good opportunities to break into top-level show jumping. The first was when Dougie Bunn, the mastermind behind Hickstead, gave him two old Grade As to compete on, which gave him some invaluable experience. The other was the offer of a job riding horses for Cecil Williams. There wasn't much of a wage along with the job, but there was, as Cecil put it, one nice horse: that horse was April Sun who, with Peter on board, was to become one of the most consistent money-winners of his era.*

It was about this time that I first remember seeing Peter compete. It was the mid-eighties, and I had just made the transition from ponies to horses. I was mainly interested in show jumping then, and Peter's horses, even the novice ones, stood out in the collecting ring because of the soft, round, easy way they carried themselves. Peter himself was his trademark unhurried but focused self, and had the look of an elder statesman of show jumping even then.

Buying and selling horses was a way of life at Cecil's, and Peter also rode for other owner-dealers such as Sue and Fred Welch. However, although the average price of a talented horse has gone up significantly since that time in the eighties, Peter feels this is more because of a change in the market, rather than a dramatic improvement in the quality of horses.

A change in the market

'I don't think the horses have got better. I can remember when I won the European Championships with La Ina – he was a big money-winner: he won £580,000 and a load of cars. We were up against the back end of Milton, Grannusch, ET, Ratina, Mon Santa, Two Step...there isn't one of those horses that wouldn't be the best in the world today. Go back a bit further and you've got Boomerang, Sportsman, Tigre. By comparison, there are no superstar horses these days.

'This is because there used to be a bigger pool of horses for the best riders to pick from. There weren't so many amateurs. Now, there are a lot of people coming in – for instance, such as syndicates and wealthy private individuals

– who buy these horses up from an early age. So a lot of the good horses are not in the right hands. Now, nine times out of ten a professional cannot afford the going rate for a world-class horse. It is extremely hard to go out and buy the horse you want. You have to produce it from an early age, or you need a bit of luck when you see a horse you want to buy, that they will agree to sell, because people don't want to do that now, either.'

TINA: *This means that Peter buys in a lot of horses at novice level to produce. However, because he spends so much time abroad competing, he has found an ingenious way of spreading the workload of training these horses.*

Developing talent

'I like to buy them in as five-year-olds and above if I can – though having said that, I've got two four-year-olds at the moment, as well as two- and three-year-olds – and I've even bred them. One I bred was placed in the World Cup qualifier at Olympia last year.

'Watching the four- and five-year-olds develop is great. Watching talent, not necessarily winning, but doing the right thing at the right time is very pleasing.

'At the moment I have a stable jockey who does a lot of the work at home and takes the young horses to smaller competitions, but because of the nature of the business, riders come and go, so I also tend to use developing riders. At the moment I use Louise Pavitt, who I think could go a long way with the right horses, further experience and training. She's one of the most natural riders to win a class that I've ever seen. Her rounds flow, and it's a pleasure to watch: but she needs the right exposure, and the right horses.

'I can always find someone to ride my horses because there are always riders around, so that's not a problem. I place horses with different riders whilst I'm away during the season to carry on the work. I prefer organizing it that way, rather than being stuck with just one rider at home, and having him ride all the horses: if I've got different horses, they suit different riders, and I place them accordingly.'

TINA: *Peter also believes that Great Britain is the best place in the world to produce young horses. One of the reasons for this is that most shows still use the traditional two-round formula for a competition; a first round from which all the clears go forward to a separate jump-off.*

This is in contrast to the format used abroad that is creeping into some shows in Great Britain, where if a horse jumps clear, they go immediately into the jump-off (a two-phase competition), therefore only going in the ring once.

The County Show circuit

'It is much better for young horses to go in the ring, jump around, come out, walk off, spend half an hour waiting for the jump-off, and go back in again. Horses grow up a lot more with that system than if they jump in a two-phase.

'Then in Great Britain, we've got the county show circuit, and the county shows are just like small international shows. I had forgotten how good they were, but last year I did the whole summer, and it was great. The horses see crowds, colours, they see cows, sheep, other horses. We won the major class at nearly every county show we did this year, and the horses came on in leaps and bounds from doing that. There is no circuit like that abroad, where horses can get exposure to that sort of atmosphere. Small international shows abroad are in little sand arenas that all look the same. We might not have all the fancy restaurants, all the fancy décor that shows abroad have, but there are a lot of nice rings, and good places to jump the horses.'

TINA: *Peter also trains riders, but puts a limit on numbers because he sees training as only part of a bigger picture.*

Buying, selling and training

'I don't find that training by itself is profitable. Where you earn the money is when the client buys the horse. And that's what I do, buy and sell the horses for

'It is much better for young horses to go in the ring, jump around, come out, walk off, spend half an hour waiting for the jump-off, and go back in again. Horses grow up a lot more with that system than if they jump in a two-phase.'

them. Then training is part of the deal. I wouldn't train any rider, ultimately, that went off and bought the horses elsewhere and just came to me for training. I'm not interested. I try to gel up the right rider with the right horse.

'I don't get a huge amount of time to train anyway, but we have had a King's Cup winner, Cameron Hanley, from this yard, and I supplied the horse as well. The same day Claudia Neureiter, also based here, won the Queen Elizabeth, so that was a good training feat.

'Naturally, the better the horses and riders are, the easier it is to train them, as long as they listen to you – but if riders won't listen to you, then you've got no chance.'

TINA: For Peter, training riders is a delicate balance between teaching them the basics in a systematic way, and preserving and developing natural feel.

Developing individual flair

'The technique of riding has changed. A lot more thinking goes into it. I remember Michael Whitaker coming to Iris's, and he got a lot of good help from her about the position of his leg and that sort of thing. Michael is a natural, but even being a natural you have to have a system and work at your game. But riders now have got quite clinical in their approach, and if you're not careful you take a lot of intuition away from the rider, and this lets them down when they go in the ring and it doesn't happen for them.

'Polework can be useful for young horses and riders, but there's a lot of trainers who will build the whole course from poles and teach the rider to ride round them. That's fine to a certain extent, but if we're talking about top class show jumping, the rider has to have, and develop, his own flair. He mustn't be so programmed that he has to practise this routine every day, because you take away from the imagination of the rider. He becomes so intent on "It has to be four strides, it has to be five"– but then what happens if the horse stumbles, or he spooks? You've got to be able to handle that, too.

'Lesser talented or experienced riders benefit from repetition training, but I do that with related distances and half strides, making things tough for them. With lesser talented riders you have to expose them to "right" situations so they learn to ride a distance correctly, but also to "wrong" situations so their mind learns how to deal with them. Half strides off corners. Long strides coming out, short strides going in. You need to do this to make up for a lack of talent, and replace it with this kind of situation, so the brain has the experience of having been there a number of times, before meeting it in the ring.

'A talented rider's reactions will see them through difficult situations. But likewise I have seen lesser talented riders, who with hard work and dedication also deal with the situation, maybe not as attractively, but with the same result as a talented rider.'

TINA: *With that in mind, I asked Peter what qualities a successful show jumper needed to possess.*

The importance of self-determination

'Without doubt the single most important quality that a successful show-jumping rider must have is self-determination in their own ability. I put that before anything, whether they've got a lot of talent or not. I've seen riders succeed who haven't been over-talented, but have had a lot of self-determination, and I've seen very talented riders dither, and if you dither at the top end it will kill you every time.

'You need self-determination to be successful in any sport, but in show jumping in particular because you are making a conscious effort for an animal as well as yourself. So I believe that your self-determination has to be even stronger than, say, a javelin thrower, because if you falter, the horse will falter. That's it. You have to ride supremely confidently to win any class now. Start dithering on a corner or a turnback, the horse loses his momentum, his rhythm, fence down, competition gone.

'That's where the rider has to be supremely confident, to transmit that confidence to the horse.'

'Without doubt the single most important quality that a successful show-jumping rider must have is self-determination in their own ability. I put that before anything, whether they've got a lot of talent or not.'

TINA: *Of course, that self-determination isn't just about winning competitions — it's also about how the riders apply themselves to all the preparation work.*

Old-fashioned horsemanship

'The biggest mistake a rider can make is to think that quick fixes and tricks can replace old-fashioned horsemanship and learning how to ride properly. Far too many shortcuts are being taken, and riders not taking the time to learn how to ride the horse in the right balance, so they have the control they need to ride the course. Having control means that the horse goes forward when the rider wants, and comes back when they want. These are the two main essentials for riding a horse in the show-jumping ring. Too many young riders coming up haven't put the effort in on the ground of working the horse in a correct manner. They haven't given the horses time to learn from their mistakes, to develop in their mind and physically in their bodies.

'I see young riders wanting a quick fix, wanting horses to jump perfectly tomorrow, and they treat the horse more as a machine rather than a partnership that will evolve over a certain amount of time with the correct riding and training. That doesn't seem to be getting through as much as it should be, and a lot of young riders fall by the wayside because of this. There is a time element in producing young riders and horses. It takes years and years, and not many are prepared to go that route, but think a bump and a bash will do the job instead.'

TINA: *Modelling himself on his early mentor, Eddie Macken, Peter is remarkable for his unflappable approach to competition, and his ability to pull a victory out of the bag. I wondered if he ever felt affected by nerves.*

Be confident in your own ability

'Anyone who says they don't get nervous is a liar, but the way they channel those nerves can have a very good effect on their performance.

'If anyone gets so nervous that they don't want to do it, then they shouldn't do it. I've seen riders white with fright, and physically sick, and if they get like that, they shouldn't do it. I don't believe your body needs to be put through that much torture just to do something that is a sport. But I get a different buzz when the trip is for medals, championships, bucketloads of money. I wake up to a certain degree.

'I believe I have great control over my nerves at competitions, and I need a nervous tension to bring out the best in me. Not that I don't get motivated: I go to work and ride my young horses round the local shows and so on. I do what's required, but I've been doing that for more than twenty years, and I can do it in my sleep.

'I still love, and will always love, the pull of a big competition such as a championships, or Calgary. I wasn't always a big Derby fan, but I enjoyed winning those three at Hickstead, and I was very cocky about it. There was no holding me back, I knew I was going to win them, and I told anyone who would listen that I would win. I was supremely confident in myself and my mare's ability to beat anyone who came along. I predicted I'd win it three times, and I did.

'Now that isn't being cocky, that's being confident in your own ability, and there are very few times in your life you can say that. I said before the Grand Prix in Calgary that I'd win it. The horse was in the form of his life, and what I said there was, if I don't make any mistakes, I know my horse won't. I knew we were faster than the rest of the field. We won the warm-up speed class on the Friday in a canter, and I couldn't see anyone to beat us.

'It's great when you've got a horse to the top of his level. I don't believe I'll be there for another year or two because the horses I've got now are all developing horses, so I'll have to keep my mouth shut for a while.'

expert insight

'Far too many shortcuts are being taken, and riders not taking the time to learn how to ride the horse in the right balance, so they have the control they need.'

TINA: *I also asked Peter where he thought show jumping could go, now there were so many good riders and horses fighting it out at the top.*

There will always be a winner

'I don't think show jumping needs to go anywhere, because you will always get a result. When you have a timed competition, you will always have a winner. It's not like dressage, where if you fall out with the judge the day before she'll go and give you a bad mark.'

TINA: *Peter cited the recent World Cup qualifier at Olympia as a case in point. There were twelve riders in the jump-off, some of them the finest in the world, including Marcus Ehning, Rodrigo Pessoa, Nick Skelton and Lars Nieberg; and yet it was won by relative outsider Richard Davenport, with two lesser known riders coming in second and third.*

No room for error

'That was a typical example of the riders coming behind him, disregarding Richard and worrying about what everyone else was going to do, and cutting each other's throats. Richard's round was a good one, but the time was very beatable. But the others tried to go so fast, that they all cocked up.

'But that is competition and you can never stop that, and you can't criticize the boys behind, because if you take that away from them, they will win nothing.

'The faster you go, the harder you go, and the smaller the room for error there is. One extra pull can be too much.

'It helps also when you have a horse who is quick from A to B, and is quick with his legs and body over a fence. That helps a lot. So a good rider will look at a very fast round, and say hang on, I can't beat that because my horse's rhythm is too slow. For instance when Calvarro, Milton and It's Otto jumped, they were not the fastest horses in the world and they couldn't compete with those quick horses off the floor, so those guys wisely rode accordingly to take second, third or fourth spot. That was the best they were going to do on the day. But there are also the times when they would outjump the rest, and then they would win. They consistently jumped a lot of clear rounds.

'Also to win, you have to have a horse that is completely in harmony with their rider. There are stages in the season when they are out of sync, maybe a little nappy, or a bit funny down their combinations, just not in full swing. But they will get into a zone when they are in top form, and when you get two or three of those in a jump-off, it's great to watch.'

TINA: *In Peter's view, there is only one significant factor that could compromise show jumping as a sport.*

Professional over amateur

'As long as the top end stays where they are and the amateur element does not buy its way through, it'll be great. If the amateur element gets in and takes over too much through paying for it, it'll destroy show jumping. As long as the top end stays professional, it'll be fine. But where a lot of the shows in Europe tend now to be 50 per cent professionals and 50 per cent amateurs, it becomes a bit of a Mickey Mouse show.'

TINA: *And as for himself?*

Doing yourself justice

'I love horses, I love the buzz of competition as long as I can do well. As long as I feel I can do myself justice, I will keep riding, and there's no age I can say, that's when I will pack up. I will retire when I get too bored of it, though I can't see that happening. I'm putting a whole string of new horses together now, and that's just as exciting as starting again.'

---

expert insight

'To win, you have to have a horse that is in harmony with their rider. There are stages in the season when they are out of sync, maybe a little nappy, just not in full swing. But they will get into a zone when they are in top form.'

Richard Davison:
Take Your Own Line

Richard Davison

Four times a World Cup finalist and winner of silver and bronze team medals at European Championships, Richard is one of Great Britain's leading dressage riders and trainers. Actively involved with the development of dressage as a sport internationally, he is also a dedicated and successful producer of young horses and riders at home, with a unique and open-minded attitude to training.

Combridge Farm is home to Richard and Gill Davison, and is the epitome of a modern competition yard. The purpose-built brick stables are laid out around three sides of a square, with archways leading to a washbox, and then down a short path to the riding arenas. The large indoor school is airy and bright, with a raised platform at one end, next to an enclosed glass-fronted sitting room, complete with sofas and a fireplace. Richard switches on an overhead gas heater as I sit myself down to watch his lesson. 'I don't believe in people getting cold,' he says.

Richard Davison has an impressive list of national and international dressage competition successes behind him: current National British Dressage Champion, four times a World Cup Finalist, winner of silver and bronze team medals at the European Championships, and last year took part in his third Olympic Games in Athens. His top-level career has spanned well over a decade – but dare I say it, he seems to be improving with age.

The rider he is working with is a young professional, sitting on a loose-limbed modern type of warmblood, a horse that is elegant and well balanced. There are advertising banners all around Richard's school, and Snap and Crackle, the two Border Collies, wander in and out of the viewing area. The bay horse is eyeing up all of this with suspicion, and although he is fairly advanced in his education – he is working at Prix St Georges level – he leaps away from the side of the school more than once.

'Remember,' says Richard, 'the spooky horse is not a stupid horse.' He goes on to explain that the rider needs to work with that intelligence and build up trust with the horse so he can use that brightness to his advantage.

He starts to use a simple exercise to counteract the horse's natural desire to run away from what scares him. As the rider approaches the 'spooky' corner, Richard asks him to make a halt, and reassure the horse. The rider softens his hand, and gives the horse a gentle pat. When the horse relaxes a touch, the rider moves him forwards and asks him with the inside leg to move a

expert insight

'Remember,' says Richard, 'the spooky horse is not a stupid horse.' He goes on to explain that the rider needs to work with that intelligence and build up trust with the horse so he can use that brightness to his advantage.

little deeper into the corner. He repeats this several times, with Richard also walking up, patting the horse whilst he is at halt, occasionally giving him a sugar lump. Each time the horse relaxes a little more, and after a few tries, softens in a much more whole-hearted way around the rider's leg.

The horse is not forced in any way to go closer to the banner, but halting him gives him a chance to accept what is there. It is vital that throughout this process, the rider remains friends with the horse. Falling out with him and putting on the pressure would only confirm the horse's worst suspicions. After the horse makes some progress in this area, they work on some changes of pace, before returning to the same exercise later. The horse is visibly better, though not 100 per cent. As Richard comments, it will take time, patience and repetition – key words for thorough training.

This consistency of purpose demonstrated by Richard was instilled in him from a young age, for although his parents had an interest in equestrianism, they lived in a town and did not own any horses. In his own words:

Natural tenacity

'I think if I hadn't been naturally keen, and pushing to get a pony, I wouldn't have had one. My parents weren't bothered if I rode or if I didn't. Having that drive to get my own pony was great, because it taught me that when you can't have something straightaway, when you have to wait for it, and work hard for it and be hungry for it, then you value it so much more than if it is just put in front of you. At the time though, I didn't enjoy it and would have much preferred to have just gone and got a pony!

'However now, if I want to get something new for the stable, or the horses, like a new solarium for instance, I really think a lot about whether I can afford it, which one will be the right one, and so on. That was the first hard lesson I learnt, but a useful one.'

> **TINA:** *Richard's tenacious attitude did not stop there. Although his parents supported him when he was riding ponies, his father often out helping him jump in the twilight after school, or analysing his riding using an early video camera, when it came to choosing a profession, Richard was persuaded to step towards something that would make him a 'proper' living. He therefore joined his father's business, and eventually was put in charge of running one of the garages connected to it. However, the garage was right in the middle of the Meynell hunting country...*

Hunting five days a week

'I got the shift patterns at the garage working so I could drive up with my Land Rover and trailer at nine o'clock to change the shifts over, sort the cash out and check everything was running smoothly. Then I'd be off on a day's hunting, back again by five o'clock, covered in mud, change over the next shift, and then go back home to sort the horses out. It worked really well to begin with, but then I started going out with more packs, in addition to the Meynell, until I was out hunting five days a week.

'My father would turn up and ask "Where is he?" Eventually he took me aside and said "Let's look at these figures for the garage." When I took over, they had been very promising, but at this stage, after six months, they were terrible. I learnt I couldn't run a business long distance. Anything you want to do, you have to have your heart in it if you want to do it successfully. My father realized my heart was in the horses, and said that then I must do that, but that I must also learn it professionally.'

TINA: *Therefore Richard started his professional life by working through the BHS system of qualifications, eventually culminating in gaining his Fellowship.*

BHS qualification

'The great thing about all these qualifications is not the exams you do, but what you learn by training for those exams. Because the syllabus was very broad, I learnt a lot of stuff that I actually still draw on today, whether it is how to deal with staff, or basic knowledge that otherwise I would perhaps only have got by tripping over it.'

TINA: *The BHS provided Richard with much of his early training, but as he became more interested in dressage, he also made several visits to the Spanish Riding School to work with Artur Kottas. In later years he trained with Klaus Balkenhol and Conrad Schumacher. Now he works mainly with his wife Gill, as his 'eyes on the floor'.*

Richard bases his training and schooling around what he calls his four-point schooling plan. This is an underlying pattern that he uses to map out both schooling sessions, and his preparation before a dressage test. It starts with a warm-up time, then works on getting the horse responsive and forward-going, is followed by practising test movements, and finishes with a cooling-off period.

expert insight

'I'm keen on a lot of suppling, because a supple horse is a willing horse. After all, if you are doing things with tight muscles it hurts, and that will affect the horse's mental state.'

Being ahead of the game

'Whatever you do, you have to have a plan, for the big picture, and the narrow focus. You need to know how you would like that plan to run, and how it actually did run. Then you compare the two. When you ride and train horses, what you've got right now is a result of what you've done previously.

'The first thing I do is say, "Well, how are you? What are you thinking, what's going on?" Then I'm keen on a lot of suppling, because a supple horse is a willing horse. After all, if you are doing things with tight muscles it hurts, and that will affect the horse's mental state. We start the suppling work by doing a lot of walk, with blankets on in the cold weather, and during this time you can see what state of mind the horse is in.

'What I try to do when I am teaching riders is to make them very aware of where they are in the four-point plan, so they don't just go through the motions of it. They need to ask themselves, whilst they are suppling the horse up, is the suppling really working today? Is the horse more stiff today because we did a lot with it yesterday? What other factors are affecting the horse? So although we follow the plan, we also really look and see how the horse is going.

'Of course, you don't always get it right, so therefore you might need to look at where you skipped or compromised on the plan. When you've put the horse away, you have a think about it, perhaps when you are driving, or at your desk, because the only way you can find out why it didn't work is to retrace your steps and look at what you did.

'This plan works for me because it gives me something to measure against. It also stops you panicking. For instance, imagine you have a five-year-old horse, which normally works beautifully at home. You take him to his first show and there are people galloping around, and you are supposed to be suppling him up, but his tail is in the air and he is snorting around. So you say to yourself, okay, usually this horse is nice and loose with about fifteen minutes work. But well, today I'll steal ten minutes from the other time to get the freshness out and the suppling in. So I know that when it comes to the time I would have spent practising test movements, I'll not bother with, say, the centre line. All this lets me be ahead of the game.

'Or with an older horse, I might have to adjust the plan in another way. Perhaps the tanks are a bit empty that day; the horse has had a long journey or isn't so fit. In that situation I would shorten the time spent in one particular section, and let the horse walk.

'So it is a plan, but you have to be aware of what is happening within each section so you see the reality of the situation.'

TINA: *Richard also gives his horses a huge amount of variety to make sure they are both mentally and physically engaged in their work. As a general rule they are schooled three times a week, hacked out, do canter work in the fields and even jump from time to time, as well as being turned out regularly. This is quite unusual in a dressage yard: in many successful yards on the continent that I have visited, the horses are lucky if they ever see the outside of the indoor school.*

Building up trust

'People think I am bonkers, especially my continental friends. They cannot believe I jump my horses, especially the expensive ones. But if you look at photographs of top sportsmen warming up, what are they doing? They're lying on the floor stretching, or hopping up and down like madmen, and are not actually playing their sport at all. We understand that they need to do a wide range of movement to exercise their muscles and motivate their brain – and that's how I feel about the horses.

'We only jump little fences with the dressage horses, but this can open up their backs more than a normal canter stride will do. Also, a lot of our horses are quite sharp and spooky, and they need to build up their courage. It's actually very helpful to put them in a situation where they look at a fence with a water tray, or a bit of plastic underneath that they are not sure about, and then you persuade them to jump it. In six years time I might be taking that horse to another artificial environment such as a big World Cup qualifier, which is like a pop concert, a completely unnatural environment for a horse. When he stands in the tunnel and says to me, I don't think we should go in there, it's too dangerous, I can communicate to him that it is okay to go, because he has trusted me in spooky situations before, and it was fine.

'Other riders build up the horse's trust in different ways, and I respect that, but the principle is the same. What concerns me is when dressage riders don't look in the horse's mind, and when they tackle problems in a confrontational way and fight with the horse, which doesn't get them anywhere. Then the horse is labelled a spooky horse and called no good, and it gets passed around and has a miserable existence.

'Of course I know there is a risk when we turn these valuable horses out, but we reduce the risk in sensible ways: we boot them up, turn them out with an old pony, or in paddocks next to each other. I do this because at the end of the day, I cannot understand how a horse standing in a stable twenty-three hours a day can have healthy muscles or a healthy mind.'

> **TINA:** This greater sensitivity to the overall needs of the horse is extending throughout the dressage world. Although Richard is not involved with the logistics of National Dressage, he is involved with the international scene, working with the FEI to mould the way forwards for dressage as a sport. At the Global Dressage Forum in 2004, the theme was 'the happy athlete', the term adopted by the FEI to set a standard for judges to measure dressage horses' performance by.

Raising awareness

'The important thing to remember is that "the happy athlete" is a general statement. If I ask myself, am I happy? the answer would be yes, but this does not mean I am deliriously happy every minute of the day! The literal interpretation of this phrase isn't what is important: what matters are the signals that it gives off.

'The best thing that's come out of it is that it raises awareness, and gets people to ask, "Are my horses happy?" It's the first time I have heard discussion between international riders and trainers about the management of horses as well as their

expert insight

'What concerns me is when dressage riders tackle problems in a confrontational way, which doesn't get them anywhere. Then the horse is labelled as spooky, called no good, and it gets passed around and has a miserable existence.'

training, and that has to be a good thing. It moves us beyond just thinking about what happens inside the white boards or how to make that half-pass better, and makes us ask, what is behind the way that horse is doing his half-pass?'

> **TINA:** Of course, there is a danger when people are learning that they take words too literally and find less-than-skilful ways around a problem. The admonition that a horse should show no resistance in his mouth, for instance, can lead to a rider cranking up the noseband to cover up that resistance. However, the reality is, that every horse will be resistant in the mouth from time to time, but what matters is whether it is a minor, temporary situation, or a more major problem that needs to be addressed in terms of the horse's schooling.

The trainer's responsibility

'There is always a need as a trainer to think about the repercussions of what you might say or do, and there is also a responsibility that stems from that. There are dangers and advantages to every schooling exercise we do, and when less experienced riders see you do something and they don't know the background to that work, it can be easily misinterpreted. I'm not so concerned about the people though, it's their horses I worry about, that their riders will go back and try something inappropriate for their level of understanding or training.

'On the other hand, we also learn through our mistakes. We all have to learn like that, but if you're smart you won't make the same mistakes I've made, or at least not for so long.'

> **TINA:** Learning from your mistakes requires a responsibility from the rider to recognize truly what is happening underneath them, and interpret what the horse is doing as feedback, rather than disobedience. This is reflected in Richard's strong emphasis on communication being a two-way situation between the horse and rider, a shift from the 'You will do what I say' techniques to a form more of 'request and response'.

How to communicate

'I think there is a tendency for riders to work too hard themselves when they are riding. The reason for this is, I believe, that the former answer to everything – be it put the horse on the bit, or make a better transition – was "Use more leg". It didn't matter what you wanted to do, that was the answer.

'The management of horses as well as their training, moves us beyond just thinking about what happens inside the white boards or how to make that half-pass better, and makes us ask, what is behind the way that horse is doing his half-pass?'

'Where we've come to now in riding is that to say "Use more leg" nowadays would be like saying "You need to communicate, so talk more". And what we actually have to do in order to communicate more is not just talk, but also listen. Not only do you have to listen, but then you need to think about that information, and try something accordingly. It's a two-way thing.

'To get people out of pushing, pushing, pushing we need to teach riders how to read the horse. On top of that, if you think of talking, how many different ways of talking are there? Different tones, phrases…we can even use silence. So when it comes to using your legs, we have to explain to riders how to use them. Maybe it's a short sharp kick that's needed here to mentally wake the horse up, or a squeeze perhaps.

'There are lots of different rhythms and strengths you can use – varying the effects according to what the horse's state of mind is at that moment in time.'

TINA: *Richard observed that this lighter type of riding has been facilitated by the type of horse that is now used in dressage. Twenty-five years ago or more, the German and Swedish warmbloods, in particular, were much heavier and 'colder' in their reactions. This often meant that they only responded to strong and heavy aids.*

Nicole Uphoff and Rembrandt: a turning point

'The huge turning point in dressage came when Nicole Uphoff and Rembrandt hit the scene. Up until then, although there were famous women dressage riders, they had male trainers or bereiters who would get on the horses and make them do it. Behind every successful female dressage rider was a very strong man. But Rembrandt was a light dancing machine, with a little girl riding him, who did it herself with her trainer on the ground. She said herself she could not ride in this way of power and strength; she had to do it in a way that worked for her, and this led the way for Isabell Werth and Anky van Grunsven. In fact, when I first went abroad to ride dressage, I didn't enjoy it very much because it seemed there was an awful lot of pressure for everyone involved.

'Another significant turning point in the last twenty years has been the way riders approach a competition mentally. With my own psychology, I tried to copy John and Michael Whitaker when I was younger and competing alongside them. John especially is so relaxed, which in turn allows him to be so sharp, and totally focused on his horse in the ring. He doesn't worry about things that are out of his control, and anyway have no bearing or influence on this moment. I am good friends with John and Michael now, and the amazing thing is that they can tell you about nearly every round of nearly every horse. The reason they can do that is because of their focus. They keep their minds uncluttered of other things.

'Narrowing your focus is something you learn to do if you want to achieve. In my life I've also learnt what are now called "distraction techniques". Before Atlanta, I was working in the outdoor school, and the indoor school was being built next door. The phone was ringing all the time, and people were coming and going to do various alterations to the place. At the end of a training session there would be a queue of people, each saying "I really need an answer, and have been here to ask you three or four times." I realized they had been asking me questions and I hadn't paid any attention to them at all.

'I didn't do it deliberately, I just knew I had to concentrate on this horse. So then I thought to myself, I've been in this bubble, and it was fantastic! – and I reflected that it would be good to train to do this a bit more!'

TINA: *Although sports psychology is a relatively new phenomenon in the horse world, ideas such as 'distraction techniques' have been used extensively in other sports to improve an athlete's focus. Those involved with sports such as shooting or archery, for instance, will train whilst they have loud rock music playing. The aim is not to ignore or fight the noise, but to let go of doing anything about it, and maintain their focus despite the noise.*

Staying focused

'My generation learnt this sort of thing by trial and error. Of course it's a bit of a shame because some people wouldn't have learnt it, and so weren't as good as they could have been. So it's good that now we have people who can

'Narrowing your focus is something you learn to do if you want to achieve. I've also learnt what are nowcalled "distraction techniques".'

tell us about these techniques, because I see riders getting distracted or angry, and you see how that affects their riding on that day.

'You just have to figure out what the most important thing is, and concentrate on that, and let all the other stuff wait.'

TINA: *The introduction of sports psychology is not the only way horse sport has changed in the last twenty years. The standard at the top has become so much higher. For instance at the 1984 Olympics, the bronze medal-winning combination scored 66 per cent. In current competition at that standard, that combination would be in about twentieth position. Also the numbers at all levels of competition have increased dramatically. This means that the best sport horses often change hands for more than a million pounds.*

There is truth in the saying that you are only as good as the horse you are sitting on, and top riders are at that level, partly because they attract good horses. However, even the expensive and well-trained horse has to be ridden with the skill to match its ability, a fact often overlooked by the less experienced, but ambitious rider.

A higher level of horsemanship

'I try to make dressage riders realize that there is a higher level of riding and looking after horses. I don't say this because I want to be a world leader, I promote it because at the end of the day I am still also a competitor, and if it did not work to think and act this way, I wouldn't do it. But it works for me, and I am sure it can work for a lot of other people, and anyway it's much more fun!

'The night before last we put up a course in the school in order to try out a show jumper for the children. We left it up, and the next day we jumped all the young dressage horses. We had four four-year-olds in the school, snorting and spooking around, and all of us were laughing our heads off. I was on the spookiest one you could imagine, but we and the horses really enjoyed it, much more than if we had just come out and done the same old thing.

'That sort of thing is about horsemanship, and it's higher than being simply a dressage rider or a show jumper.'

> **TINA:** *The other area of concern for Richard is that with so many riders having the narrow focus of wanting to be on teams and to ride at Olympic level, there are not so many riders around to produce young horses for this market.*

An international problem

'This problem of who is going to ride and produce the young horses is not just a problem in Great Britain, it's a problem everywhere, even in Germany and Holland, where they have a fantastic professional riders' system.

'Nowadays, everyone wants to be a show jumper or a dressage rider, and they want to cut into that straightaway. They don't want to ride the three-year-olds that might be bronco-ing around. It's harder and harder to find people who will ride these horses, and who know that the three-year-old isn't trying to get you off, it's just that the girth is a bit tight, or he's a bit fresh.'

> **TINA:** *By avoiding this type of work, younger riders are not only missing out on a valuable element of their education, they are also, certainly in Richard's eyes, missing out on a business opportunity.*

The significance of marketing strategy

'I had one young jumping rider here the other day, and I told him that he needed to pay attention to his horse's walk. He asked me how was

expert insight
'Get your head round the fact that this is a business just like any other, and that you have to be able to train nice horses for ordinary people to ride. If you can do that, you can generate the income to buy the horses that will enable you to be a good competition rider.'

that going to make the horse jump better? I said, well, it is not going to turn a moderate jumper into a good jumper, but there is one way you could look at it, if you need a reason: you told me that you were giving this horse six months, and if it didn't improve, you were going to sell it. Now, this horse is quite a nice mover, but if you have wrecked his walk, you won't be able to sell him as a dressage horse. So actually you need to learn what the market is for dressage, even if only in a small way, so you don't lose too much on this horse. Because if you lose money on this horse, you can't buy a better jumper, and without horses you can't be a competitive show jumper. This is where you need to think beyond whether you can get four or five strides down a distance. The modern rider has to have more of marketing and business strategy.

'You cannot do this game without some money. I don't mean you have to be driven by money, but something has to pay the bills. If you can, get your head round the fact that this is a business just like any other, and that you have to be able to train nice horses for ordinary people to ride. If you can do that, you can generate the income to buy the horses that will enable you to be a good competition rider.'

TINA: *Richard would like to promote that producing young horses can also be fun and satisfying, as well as meeting a gap in the market.*

An alternative goal

'At international level, this is beginning to be addressed by having the Young Horse Championships. This will encourage people back into producing young horses well, because to win the Five-Year-Old Championships you need to know how to start a horse off in a good way. It is also an alternative to having an Olympic dream: maybe that won't happen, but this other championships will give riders an alternative goal.'

TINA: *Some people in the horse world are horsemen; some are good at making a business. Richard not only manages to be both, but he also has fun in the process. He has taken the best from a variety of teachers, and with his own innate common sense, has made a competitive and business success of his life.*

Supersede the ordinary

'I've never worried about following the crowd. When I am helping younger trainers and riders now, I say all right, if you want to be normal, that's fine, but don't expect to be an outstanding competitor because you have to always have your head above the crowd, you have to be different, or you will be ordinary. So don't ever be worried about doing the same as everyone else. You have to look, you have to question everything, and evaluate what you see. That's what I've done, and when I go to my grave, I'll be able to say, this was the way I was happiest working.'

Robert Dover
& the Path to Excellence

Robert Dover

A six-time Olympian, Robert is one of the most knowledgeable and articulate dressage riders in the world. A flamboyant showman and a dedicated trainer, he is as passionate about dressage now as when he first started out. The force behind the Developing Rider Programme in the USA, he is a person who brings a touch of magic both when he rides and when he is teaching his students.

They call him 'Mr Dressage' in America, and not surprisingly, for watching a gaggle of riders preparing for the Grand Prix Freestyle at the first CDI*** of the season in Wellington, Florida moving with such peace and fluidity are a sharp contrast to the mostly effortful and obvious work that is going on around them.

Robert Dover has competed at six Olympic Games, winning a team bronze medal at three of them, and has been America's leading dressage rider and trainer for more years than anyone cares to remember. Today, he and Kennedy give the kind of performance that draws you in as a spectator, leaves you wanting it to go on forever, because the horse performs his work with so much ease and flair. It engages me on a completely different level. Yes, I have an intellectual respect for the technical correctness, but more than that, I appreciate it as an artistic, enjoyable and inspiring display of harmony in horsemanship.

It is all the more remarkable that he can give such a performance, bearing in mind that Robert retired from competition after the Olympic Games in Sydney because of back problems: six damaged discs and sciatica down one leg, which he compares to having an ice pick dug into his thigh. He only returned to competitive riding in time for Athens because his long-time owner and supporter Jane Clark bought the elegant Kennedy for him not long before the Games. Despite this, the combination swept the board at the US selection trials, and went on to win a bronze team medal, and gain a placing in the top ten in both the Freestyle and the Grand Prix Special.

Though many riders lay claim to being from a certain school of riding, Robert has travelled far and wide in his pursuit of excellence. He started off in the Pony Club in the Bahamas and Florida, and made his way up the grades culminating in passing his 'A' test. When he was fifteen, he was fortunate enough to meet Colonel Lundqvist, a Swedish cavalry officer, an Olympic fencer and also a dressage rider, who had moved to the States in the seventies and trained the US dressage team.

Early training

'Colonel Lundqvist took me under his wing. I went to Maryland where he was working at Linda Zang's farm, and I stayed with him till he died in the eighties.

'He was an incredibly wonderful man. He was a person of great morals and ethics, and made this indelible imprint on my mind as to how horses should be treated and how riding should be done, both from a practical standpoint and basic good horsemanship. He would say things like "The gates to brilliance are surrounded by a cloud of sweat and tears", and "Art ends where violence begins", which we had painted on a wall at the farm.

'When Colonel Lundqvist died I went to work with a lady in Maryland, and I had an older horse that taught me a lot, called Lago Majiore. It had been trained by Willi Schultheiss, so when Schultheiss came to America, I trained with him for a week and he suggested that I come to Germany where he would help me. I was lucky enough to do this, a couple of years later.'

TINA: *There were definite contrasts in the ways Colonel Lundqvist and Willi Schultheiss trained the young Robert. Not only were they from slightly different schools of thought, but there were other, logistical obstacles to overcome.*

Understanding the horse's mechanics

'Colonel Lundqvist was about standing and giving you daily, methodical lessons. You did your warm up, long. Then you did your part of the ride that was about making the animal elastic forward and back, using what he called a "rubber band" exercise. The horse had to go forward and collect, lengthen and collect on a circle. Then you would go on and learn certain lessons.

'Schultheiss was a genius of a rider. He would get on a horse that looked as if it was built like a post-and-rail fence, and within a minute it took on the most unbelievable shape. I would watch, and because I didn't speak German, I would take in by osmosis how he worked and what he did. I was mesmerized by the fact that this man could get on any horse and produce animation that I had never seen before. Riding his horses gave me the feeling of that kind of thing, but it wasn't that I was getting a formal education like I did from Colonel Lundqvist.

'I was very fortunate in my career, because I went from Schultheiss to Georg Theoderescu, to Reiner Klimke and then Herbert Rehbein. Rehbein was a disciple of Schultheiss and in the same mould. I remember at eleven-thirty one night he had been drinking, and he yelled out to one of the guys, "Bring me that horse!" It was three years old, and he got on it in his street clothes. He cantered it for a few seconds, did a flying change, then another, and then he did twenty one-times. That's the kind of a rider who could get on and was able to go into the mechanics of the horse and create things because of this amazing sense of feel and timing he possessed.

'It wasn't training, it just happened. If you watch someone do that, you might think to yourself "Well, that's a mystery" – but it's really not. It's a simple notion that you can, when you understand the horse's mechanics, figure out how to get it to go from this lead to that lead.'

TINA: *Like most trainers, Robert has his own particular way of expressing the basic concepts that a horse and rider need to grasp, that are the vital foundation for more advanced work.*

A set of objective rules

'The first thing is that in any art, you have a set of objective rules, which creates what is called a craft. So, everyone can learn their craft, and the basic principles are that the horse first has to be moving forwards off the driving aids. Secondly, the horse has to move straight, so he is straight on straight lines and bent on bent lines, so his hind feet follow in the tracks of his front feet on the same side. Thirdly, once he is moving forward and straight, which allows him to create the bend and the straight lines, the outside rein is married with those other two sets of aids to create, within the length and time of a breath, a half-halt.

'By breathing in and closing the legs, the horse wants to bend more and speed up: but the rider closes the outside rein at that second. This closes an imaginary door in the horse's face, and says "No, you're not allowed to speed up or bend more" – but his hind legs are still being pressed forwards.

'So at that second the horse, having yielded to the action of the outside hand, still bends his hindlegs more, so his croup lowers, and the forehand raises. But because he has yielded to the outside hand, the horse raises from the wither, and that creates the beautiful arch.

'That is all done within the inhale, then the rider has to reward that, so by exhaling, the relaxing of that braced and driving seat, and the relaxing of the outside hand, the horse is allowed to resume his forward progress again, in a new state of balance and attention. The inhale is the dictation, and the exhale is the reward. So all my horses learn the marriage of those three sets of aids.

'Then we start with the idea of creating energy through the inhale part of the half-halt, and directing that energy whatever way we want. That's what causes the movement to happen. So you have a beautiful package of aids that allows you to create all these movements by changing the weight of the horse, and creating energy with collection, and then directing it.

'It's a bit like the Wizard of Oz, when the Wicked Witch created a ball of energy in her hand and then threw it at the scarecrow. You are collecting this swirling and self-propelling energy of the horse, and then you direct it and it flies through the air. This is what you see when dressage is happening beautifully. Like the conductor of a fabulous orchestra with a tiny baton.'

TINA: *This metaphor of the half-halt as a 'breath in and out' is a beautiful and effective one, especially for describing the two phases of it. Many riders get hung up on the half-halt, not realizing that it is a means to an end, not an end in itself.*

Understanding the half-halt

'The half-halt is the doorway through which we make every change of pace, gait, movement and of balance. What happens is that riders don't understand where the half-halt comes from, and so they pluck the idea out of the air and say, "Well, you know what that is."

'But so many times people don't know that it comes from the driving aids, the two legs and the seat, and the bending aids, the two legs and the inside rein, and the third set of aids, the outside rein. Married together, these create the half-halt. Then the quantity of each of those sets of aids, how much seat, versus how much leg, versus how much rein, creates the difference in each of those half-halts, and that creates different directions of energy into each movement that you perform.

'The thing is, you could go to that warm-up arena today, where there were how many riders, riding at FEI level, and if you went and did a survey of how many of them truly understood what they were doing, who had dissected it down to that most basic idea and understood it, and actually then, if they were trainers, taught that, I think you would find that actually very few know what they are doing, and also know the "whys" of what they are doing.'

TINA: It is this part of riding education that can take so much time. It is one thing to feel it, and another to understand something and be able to repeat it time and again, on a number of different horses. But in order to even feel what is going on in the first place, Robert stresses that the rider must have a well-established seat.

The well-established seat

'It is very difficult for a rider to feel things if they have not taken the steps to produce in themselves a truly independent and balanced seat. If you are gripping to stay on something that is moving, you cannot feel other little very subtle nuances that you would want to feel in an animal. You have to have a balanced and independent seat before you start to feel things. That is why part of the craft of learning to ride is that you have to go all through the steps, which may include being lunged for long periods of time, it may include many, many hours, months, years of training to produce a harmonious seat. Once the rider has that sort of seat, only then can they truly start to help a horse become the best that it can become.

'Then when a rider sits well, the best way to help them become more aware of what they are feeling is to let them sit on a horse that is so wonderful in what it does that it allows them to feel things that they would not normally feel.'

TINA: Training is one thing, but the challenge for all competitive riders is to be able to produce work in the arena that is as good as it is on the best days at home. Like many competitions, dressage can be won or lost in the warm-up, before the rider even goes through the white boards.

Getting to the arena at the right moment

'I look at every horse as an individual, and I try to figure out what is the best way to bring them to the exact right point as I go toward the arena. If you talk to any dressage rider, they will tell you that that is actually the hardest part of our sport, getting to the arena at the right moment without having overdone it or underdone it.

'With Kennedy, I have to trust a great deal that he is going to have the good intentions that he does when he goes to the ring. Sometimes I underestimate – that's what I did the day before yesterday – I underestimated how much he still had in him, got to the ring, and when the camera shutters went off we went

'Talk to any dressage rider and they will tell you that getting to the arena at the right moment, without having over- or underdone it, is the hardest part of our sport.'

flying through the air. But it was his first time out since the Olympics, so I patted him at the end because he had fun, he just was a little too wild. But today he was pretty much right on.'

TINA: *This day, about twenty minutes before the test, I watched Robert in the warm-up arena. Kennedy displayed one of the most relaxed walks I have seen in a Grand Prix dressage horse. He was collected, but had plenty of length in his neck, and with every stride seemed to have all the time in the world. Then Robert picked up the reins a little more, struck off to canter and, after a short while, asked him for an extension; then collected him again and asked for a canter pirouette. The horse performed it well, and within seconds was back in walk, as settled as he had been before Robert asked him for that movement from the test, walking out, his ears in that half-way position, occasionally nudging towards Robert and then nudging forwards.*

Gauging how much more to do

'I gauge how much more I need to do by what I feel. I see it as, okay I've got twenty more minutes, this is what I am feeling, I think I will walk for five.'

TINA: *Then in the last minutes, Robert started to ask a little more, building up a bit more suspension in the horse. In response the horse started to gain a little in his stride, get a bit more onwards, and in response he got a friendly shake of the rein, as if to say 'Hey, you know this, wait a second!' And as soon as he responded to that correction, he got relaxation again.*

'Don't forget the brakes'

'I said to him, this is where I want to bring you back to where you are really lively, thinking forward on light aids, but also where I feel like I have some brakes. Because with Kennedy, a lot of times, once you get him very forward, the hard part is he can lose his brakes. So I have to say, "Don't forget forward, but don't forget the brakes, either!"'

> **TINA:** *Finally came the test itself. Robert entered in a brave canter, and after making his salute to the judges, turned right at C. Kennedy had a slight spook as he passed M, coming across the diagonal in extended trot; Robert then eased the curb rein as he came into the passage. To me, Robert had felt that little bit of tension in the horse and had just eased off the pressure so that instead of the steam building up, he gave the horse a moment to relax.*

Riding passage

'When Kennedy comes to passage and really collects himself, if you have too much curb he can get himself a little behind the vertical. So rather than let that happen, I soften up the curb and let him stay on the snaffle rein. I consciously say to myself, Robert, lower your hand and let him do it.

'If I stay out of his way, and help him balance, that's all I have to do.'

> **TINA:** *When it comes to riding the test, there is a lot a rider can do to make the difference between winning and losing. Some riders are natural showmen, some need a few tips.*

Showmanship

'There are so many ways to gain points. Of course you tailor it to every horse and rider, what will be the best way of presenting it. For instance, if you have a horse who has a nice medium trot, but not overwhelming, I tell that rider when they do their medium trot, to do the biggest extended trot they can possibly do. Then when they need to show their extended trot, they know that they are not going to get a bigger trot than that medium trot. So what I tell them to do is turn the corner, sit up a little taller, and make their eyes very big. So the judges see the look on their face, and think from their expression that it is going to be even bigger than the last medium. That's showmanship.

'Then a rider might ask me, what if the judge says it's not different? And so I say, Well, here's the thing: if you do less in a medium trot, they say not enough and give you a six. Then you do more in the extensions and they say, that looks more like a medium, and give you a seven. On the other hand, if you do the greatest trot you can for your medium and get an eight, and then you do basically the same for your extension, with your eyes big, and the judges say well, it wasn't really that different and they give you a seven, well that's an eight and a seven that makes fifteen, as opposed to a six and a seven that makes thirteen.'

TINA: *Another part of the equation is that in order for the horses to give their best, they need to be in the finest physical shape possible.*

The 'happy athlete'

'I have a wonderful team of people who work with me, and we all make the horses and their health our number one priority. Every single day we look at them, feel them, take their temperatures, know where they are…if something is beginning to happen with one of the horses, we catch it early on because we live them, we know what they are thinking and feeling all the time.

'It's very difficult to do this sport without injury. Many times, the better the animal does it, the more wear and tear it causes. Every extended trot is like water out of the well. However, with Kennedy in particular, I am really lucky. This is an animal who's known all his life that he is loved. It makes an enormous difference, because his attitude about life is so incredibly positive. Also he is a naturally well built horse and that makes him able to perform these movements without stress to his body. This is partly why at the Global Dressage Forum they named him the second most "happy athlete".'

TINA: *Inevitably, in this conversation about keeping the horses happy and working them in a fair way, our conversation turned to the subject of outline, and whether horses should be worked in a 'deep' way, that is, with a lower neck carriage and their noses behind the vertical. This is a debate that rages constantly in the dressage world, with misunderstandings of what a rider or trainer might be trying to achieve by working a horse in such a way, when the 'classical' definition is that the horse should work with his poll as the highest point and his nose at, or just in front of, the vertical.*

Being 'on the aids'

'The thing about riding is that people create an idea in their mind that classical means this, or classical means that, and if you ride a horse in this frame or that frame, it's not productive or good for the horse.

'Whether you are creating a parallelogram or a heart shape out of the horse, the question is, are you producing the most athletic, comfortable and happy animal possible with that kind of training?'

But at the end of the day, a horse that is completely on the aids is a horse that is one hundred per cent adjustable at the will of the rider.

'This means that if you choose, you can bring his carriage down to where his nose is between his knees, or you can choose to bring him above the vertical, or you can choose to put him anywhere in between…. and also you can choose to put his hindlegs underneath him in relation to that. Whether you are creating a parallelogram or a heart shape out of the horse, the question is, are you producing the most athletic, comfortable and happy animal possible with that kind of training?

'Whether a rider is skilled enough to do this, or if certain individual techniques will work for other riders, is a whole different thing, because that is to do with feeling again. However, there are many trainers who always keep the horses on the bridle, they don't even stretch their horses, and I will tell you that a horse trained in that sort of way is much more difficult to ride. The horses also lose the desire to go forward because their backs become so stiff.'

TINA: *As Robert pointed out earlier, to reach a point where a rider is skilful enough to ride a horse with such feeling, can take a very long time and a great deal of application. He attributes his own longevity in the sport almost entirely to the attitude he has cultivated throughout his life.*

Going for the 'long haul'

'When I was a kid, I was always extremely inquisitive, and very disciplined. That was my nature as a child. Those two things together meant that from an early age I wanted to understand – it wasn't enough for me to just do it, I wanted to know how. When I was thirteen and living in the Bahamas there was a girl who had imported a horse from Germany. It went in a completely different way to my horse, and I didn't understand that, and I wanted to know what that was about, so I asked my trainer and went round and around trying to figure it out. That's the way I've always been.

'I really love this sport, and I really love my horses, and when I'm teaching, I love my students. It comes from that. When you do it from that place, you have the energy to keep going.

'When young riders come to me now, looking for advice, I tell them to get the nicest possible horse they can, and go to the best trainer they can, and settle in and go for the long haul. Stay really true to that line. If riders think that the ribbon is more important than the quest for being the very best that they can be, then people get so ambitious that they forget the best interests of the horse many times. They jump over rungs in the ladder and leave things out.

'The beauty of our sport and our art is that it allows someone to find out more about who they are in relationship to the horse, through the medium of this wonderful animal that we love, but that we also use to find those things out.

'As long as you have a really super trainer and a nice horse, then things will start to work out for you, and you will start to look at the road as being the thing that brings you joy every day. I was talking to a young lady today, and she was talking about wanting to go to the World League Finals. I said, you know what, you are a really good rider, you have a really nice horse, make your goal to be as great as you possibly can with your horse and the other things will be by-products of that. But if you make the World League Finals the most important thing, then what happens is that you make errors in judgement as to what to do next, where to compete next, where to present yourself next.

'I always tell people, if you are riding well on a good horse, you should be going down every centre line to be the greatest, to show everyone how fabulous you are, and the by-product will be the blue ribbon or making a team.

'So I always say to myself before I go down a centre line, "Robert, let's have an incredibly fun time." And you know what? The hell with the judges or anyone who is watching, I'm just going to go in with my horse that I love and have an incredibly fun time, and everything else will sort itself out.

'Before this Olympics, the guys who made my freestyle had to remind me of that. Right after Aachen they called me and said "Robert, you were not having a good time," which I knew. They told me I was worrying too much about everything, and told me I had got to say, in other words, screw it, and go have a fun time. So that's what I did, down the next three centre lines and on to the Olympics. Just went and had an amazing time.

'But if you don't think that way, it can be heart-breaking in the end, and counter productive to the horse's well-being. If you don't really love the road, it can be a real disaster for people.'

TINA: *Settling in for the long haul has been a mainstay of Robert's life, and I asked him if he had ever been tempted to take shortcuts, or change the philosophy he developed under the guidance of Colonel Lundqvist and his other mentors.*

'Art ends where violence begins'

'There have been times when I have veered away from that, only to find out, sometimes in a very obvious way, that I should not have, and then I came back to my grounding. Things in my life have kept telling me how important it is to look at horses in the way I do, as opposed to saying "I've got to do this, or I've got to do that."

'Like anybody who's worth anything with horses, I have had some very big ups and some very big downs. I've had some of the worst rides of my life at some of the most important times in my life, and if anything, it probably gave me a better perspective of what it all is. Within the whole range of my career, which has been a long time now, I would say I keep coming back to Colonel Lundqvist's sayings, "The gates of brilliance are surrounded by a cloud of sweat and tears", and "Art ends where violence begins".'

TINA: *Robert himself admits that he is on borrowed time when it comes to competing. The treatment for his back only brings him relief from the pain intermittently, and riding when he cannot give his best any more does not suit him. Nevertheless, he will continue to be the guiding light behind the Developing Rider Programme in the United States, and train others with his customary enthusiasm. And with his latest project, as judge for a reality TV programme to find a rising dressage star, I have no doubt that whatever his role in the equestrian world, Robert will still be having an 'incredibly fun time'.*

Henrietta Knight:
Stay True to What You Believe in

Henrietta Knight

Immersed in horses since she was born, Henrietta is a horsewoman in the traditional sense. Throughout her life she has ridden, trained and bred horses for a variety of spheres, and has now emerged as one of the leading steeplechase trainers in Great Britain. Particularly noted from having trained Best Mate, three times the winner of the Cheltenham Gold Cup, she has an incredible ability to pick out the finest young racehorses when they are little more than gangly youngsters in the rough, and has the dedication to training that would rival any top sportsman.

A t the age of six I made the leap from hobbyhorse to a real pony, when the Knight family lent me a Shetland called Augustus for the summer holidays. Apparently, when I was not riding him, I led Augustus everywhere, even wanting to take him in the house. When I was older, I rode Connemara ponies belonging to Henrietta and her mother, in working hunter pony classes and show-jumping competitions. As an adult, I schooled racehorses from her yard that came to Waterstock for extra jump training.

This means that I have made many visits to West Lockinge Farm in the past, and as I drove into the tiny village again I remembered the thought that always hit me as we delivered horses and ponies back and forth: if I did not live at Waterstock, then I would dearly love to live here. Today, as I park amongst the converted farm buildings, watched by several elegant heads, that thought has changed ever so slightly. Now I think to myself, were I a racehorse, I would want to be trained by Henrietta Knight.

West Lockinge Farm was never meant to be racing yard. There are no long lines of identical stables, or square courtyards. Instead there are clusters of loose boxes, some in barns, others tucked into various corners. The horses stabled along the outside of the yard have upper doors cut into the walls of their stables so they can look out over the village. Others have windows in the partitions between the stables so they can see each other. Bantams, ducks and chickens wander around the yard.

I have arrived a few minutes early on purpose. I wanted time to look over some stable doors, because one of the things that stands out about Henrietta is that she trains some of the best looking and well put-together horses in the racing world. She has the gift of being able to pick out a good horse, from the Connemaras she breeds, to the hunters she judges in the summer months, and most successfully of all, the steeplechasers she sources and trains. To date those horses have won nearly six hundred races, including the triple Cheltenham Gold Cup winner, Best Mate.

An eye for a horse

'I think you either have an eye for picking a horse, or you don't. You can develop that eye by the way you've been brought up with horses. For me it goes back to the days that I was with your father: he had a wonderful eye for a horse, and he always kept things simple. He wanted a horse that was balanced, a horse that drew forward, and one that was an athlete.

expert insight

'I want a horse that's nice and square over its legs, and balanced, and especially for our game, they do need to jump. We see a lot of young horses jump loose before we buy them.'

'I want a horse that's nice and square over its legs, and balanced, and especially for our game, they do need to jump. We see a lot of young horses jump loose before we buy them, and many get discarded because their technique isn't good enough, even for steeplechasers.'

TINA: *Henrietta buys very few horses from the big National Hunt sales at Fairyhouse or Doncaster. She prefers to rely on her contacts in Ireland to alert her to horses that might be of interest, and this means she often buys from the breeders, or watches potential purchases run in a point-to-point. Unlike buying from a sale, when the only way to assess the horse is by watching it walk and trot in hand, this gives her a chance to see the horses in action and gives her more idea of their capabilities. Although she pays some attention to bloodlines, she puts the conformation and performance of the horse first.*

What to look for

'I like a horse to have a big eye. Quite often I'll walk into a yard and see the horse looking over the door, and I just won't like its head. Apart from anything, it's also difficult to sell the horse to an owner if it has a mean look in its eye and its ears are back.

'Both the foreleg and the hind leg are important. I would hate to buy a horse that is back at the knee. I also like them to have a fairly level back, not one that is dipped. I want the horse to have their hind legs underneath them, and to use their hind legs in an active way when they move. I especially like them to have a good walk, one where they overtrack, and really use their shoulder. If they walk well, they usually gallop well.

'There are certain times you have to let go, though. Some stallions don't move well themselves, yet throw good racehorses. Deep Run, for instance, was one of the most successful sires of all time, yet his stock had terrible action. If there is a stallion that is throwing offspring that are winning, and they have a particular trait, like being short in the walk, or swinging a leg in trot, you have to let go of it.

'Occasionally we will also let one of our principles go if we are buying a horse from a point-to-point. If he looks very special, but is not perfect in his conformation, turns a foot out or is a bit long in the pastern perhaps, we let it go if he has an engine.

'Because Best Mate is by Un Desperado, who was by Top Ville, I've tended to support anything with Top Ville in its lineage, because he has had such a strong influence over the jumpers. But it is difficult, because by the time you buy these horses, and they start to do well at the age of seven or eight, the stallions are dead.'

TINA: *Much of the inherent horse sense and appreciation for a good stamp comes from Henrietta's upbringing. Her mother Hester rode all her life, and built up a successful Shetland pony stud; her father rode several winning point-to-pointers, and was secretary to the Old Berks Hunt. Henrietta and her sister Ce spent the summers competing in Pony Club competitions, and the winters hunting the ponies and point-to-pointers.*

Lockinge is close to the heart of British steeplechasing, Lambourn, so it is no surprise that it was also home to Reg Hobbs, who trained Battleship, the only stallion ever to win the Grand National, in 1936. Henrietta spent many valuable hours watching him work with horses, and hacking her pony out with him, listening to his stories of racing and training. It was Reg Hobbs who talked her uncle into turning a disused tennis court into a loose jumping school, which she still uses today. Henrietta also rode out for a local trainer from the age of fourteen, and even trained a donkey, together with her sister, to win the local Donkey Derby. After she left school, before training to become a teacher, Henrietta evented extensively, the highlight of her career being a twelfth placing at Badminton in 1973, on Blitzkrieg.

Although she taught history and biology for four years, horses were still Henrietta's main priority. Gradually she began to build up a livery yard, breaking and training young horses, especially for local racehorse trainer, Captain Tim Forster. It was Captain Forster that Henrietta accompanied on horse-buying trips to Ireland, and gradually, as he became older and even more nervous of flying, he let Henrietta go by herself, to look at horses and report back to him. During this time, Henrietta made many contacts with horse agents and old-fashioned Irish horsemen, in whose presence she learnt even more about what made a good horse.

It is this sort of knowledge and experience, infused from an early age, that has helped Henrietta develop a highly individual method of training racehorses. Her horses do not go out in long strings to the same gallops every day, as most racehorses do: instead, they do their slow fittening work round the roads, woods and estate that surround Lockinge, usually in pairs or small groups.

An individual way of training racehorses

'I think a lot of it goes back to my time eventing and breaking in young horses, the type of training that never included going out in big groups. When you see horses in big strings in places like Newmarket, they go blindly nose to tail, which may suit flat horses because they only need to walk along like that and then go up the gallops as fast as they can. But the jumpers need to be able to use their brains and enjoy life, not be like zombies.

'I think our way is more interesting for them, and it is certainly more interesting for the staff. I plan what routes they will take, and then Terry and I drive around looking for them, to see how the horses are working. It keeps everyone awake and they can't take short cuts, because we know where they are supposed to be. The horses are happier, and it suits the environment, especially as we live on an estate.'

TINA: 'Terry Biddlecombe is Henrietta's husband and training partner of more than ten years. Although she was previously a successful trainer in her own right, there is no doubt that Terry, three times Champion Steeplechase Jockey, and winner of more than 900 races, is an integral part of what has propelled the stable into the big time. As a former jockey, noted for his beautiful hands and highly competitive streak, Terry is well equipped to advise the jockeys how to ride a race, as well as directing the training of the horses in the jumping paddock, and helping Henrietta monitor the horses whilst they are working around the estate. He is also a laid back, if tough-minded personality, which complements Henrietta's highly superstitious nature.

Husband and wife team

'I couldn't do it on my own. You need someone to talk to, to be a buffer. Terry has such a depth of knowledge, and sees things that I miss.

'The family that we buy from in Ireland, the Costellos, consists of a father and five sons. Tom, the father, once said that they worked together as a team, because if you go to a sale and you've got four eyes looking at an animal rather than two, you are far less likely to buy the wrong one. And it's true, if you're doing it together as a team, it does help. I know people who do it on their own, but it does help to have a back-up. You can so easily miss something in the heat of the moment.'

> TINA: *Getting the horses fit to race, and having them peak at the optimum moment, involves a steady and consistent programme of work that builds up stamina, muscle tone and cardio-vascular fitness.*

The racehorse's holiday

'When you start from scratch it takes about ten to twelve weeks to get the horses fit, before they even get on a racecourse, particularly because we still have this very English tradition of them having a holiday in the field in the summer. Firstly, it has always been done that way, and secondly it's cheaper for the owners, because they have two months when they are not having to pay full training fees. Thirdly, it used to be that the staff would go for a holiday and would not be around to ride them.

'In the perfect world, though, I don't think I would ever turn the horses out completely, but instead would bring them in at night. We do that with Best Mate and some of the others, because it means you can keep an eye on them all the time. Sometimes it breaks your heart, you turn them out looking absolutely superb, and then when you get them back in they've got an awful grass belly, and their necks have gone, and you have to start the whole process again. After all, you wouldn't send an athlete off to lie on the beach and eat strawberries and cream for two months, so why give a horse that sort of holiday?

'The horses that have had the kind of holiday that Best Mate gets, out in the day and in at night, get fitter much quicker, and they don't lose their muscle tone.'

> TINA: *Traditional fittening methods usually include a substantial period of walking, but Henrietta has adapted this for her own purposes.*

An individual work routine

'When we get the horses back in we don't walk them for very long. The old-fashioned idea of just walking them comes from the days when you got very fat hunters in from the field that could hardly do anything except walk.

> 'If they have been out in the field, they have been trotting and cantering every day. Then if you stable them all the time and just walk them you have a bomb on your hands.'

'I think if they have been out in the field, they have been trotting and cantering every day. Then if you stable them all the time and just walk them you have a bomb on your hands. The staff get bored, walking for miles, and they sit on them in the same place in the saddles, and then you get sore backs. So we tend to walk them for a couple of days, and then introduce some trot work.

'After a couple of weeks we introduce some gentle canter work. They do some walk and trot, canter two or three furlongs, and then continue for a bit of a hack. Obviously if a horse has had leg trouble, we wouldn't canter him for perhaps six weeks, just stick to walking and trotting.

'There's a lot less roadwork and slow work done with racehorses in general nowadays, and there are several reasons for this. Firstly, the economics of it all: it is time-consuming and labour-intensive. Then a lot of training yards do not have places that they can do slow exercise, especially when the roads can be so dangerous now. In fact this means that many of the yards don't do any roadwork at all.'

TINA: *At West Lockinge, some of this traditional roadwork is replaced with schooling work on the flat, riding the horses in a round outline similar to a riding horse, and teaching them the rudiments of steering, stopping and moving forwards. This is done with both the younger and the more experienced horses.*

Flatwork for the racehorse

'It is especially good to do some flatwork if an older horse has got a bit set in his ways, has been hanging in a race, or has become one-sided. The older horses can get a little cunning and a bit set, not using themselves the way they should, and so it helps if they can be squared up on the flat.'

TINA: *In addition to this more 'event' type of training, Henrietta also does more jump schooling than the average racehorse trainer. The young horses are loose jumped,* and then introduced to the range of small, inviting cross-country fences, such as log piles and pheasant feeders, that inhabit the jumping paddock. Later on they are trained over hurdles and steeplechase fences. As a general rule, Henrietta likes to give the chasers three good schools at the beginning of the season, and has even been known to give a seasoned campaigner like Best Mate a jump, close to a major race. She believes it not only keeps the horses tuned up, but the jockeys as well.

Henrietta has a gentle gallop on the farm, but for some of their faster work, the horses are boxed up or hacked over to nearby steeper gallops, on the woodchip at David Gandolpho's, or the old turf at Mick Channon's.

A varied training routine

'Other trainers would disagree with me, and say you want to do the same thing every day. Martin Pipe's theory is that if you do something different, it upsets the horses because it is out of their routine. He believes that because horses are creatures of habit, they like to know exactly what they are doing every day, and if they know that, they eat well, settle and get into a system, whereas if you put them in a box and take them to a new place to gallop, it upsets them.

'However, I think it is very good for them to go in a horsebox to a new place. After all, they have got to travel to the races.'

TINA: It is interesting that you can have two trainers, each with equally viable theories, which result in many winners in practice. It is true that horses are creatures of habit, and benefit from a consistent routine. However, it is also true that horses benefit from a change to that routine in order to stay fresh and interested.

At West Lockinge, this consistency is provided by a regular stable routine, where the horses are fed at the same time every day, and also go out to work at a similar hour. The logistics of the horse's individual work programmes are recorded in a workbook, which Henrietta fills out herself, every day.

Everything is recorded

'I write each horse's work in the workbook, and then it is photocopied and given out to everyone in the yard. Then everyone knows what they are doing. We also have a medical book, and any kind of medical treatment that is given to the horses is written in that. Andy Fox, the head lad, writes anything extra that the horses get in his book, and then all the books are put together.'

'It is especially good to do some flatwork if an older horse has got a bit set in his ways, has been hanging in a race, or has become one-sided.'

TINA: *The medical book plays a vital part in the monitoring of each horse's progress, for closely tied in with the need to get the horses racing fit is the ever-present concern of keeping them sound. Like most human athletes who are also pushing themselves close to their limits, fitness does not always equal healthiness, and the possibility of any number of injuries is high.*

The worst side of training

'Whatever happens, you can't stop them hurting themselves. It's the worst side of training, having to tell the owners when the horse has hurt itself. This year we have had so many injuries, and for the most extraordinary reasons. The things that horses can do, even in the stable, are frightening.

'We do our best to train horses on nice surfaces at home, but then you go to the races and the horse is running in the seventh race on chopped-up ground, or they get knocked into in a race, or fall, and that is when they hurt themselves.

'It's a long process, you've got to find the horses, buy them, and then one of them makes you think you've got the right horse. You get it to its peak, and then it gets injured. It is heartbreaking when that happens to one you've got close to the top. And the trouble is, the closer you get to a big race, the more pressure there is on every aspect of the horse, and the more likely it is that something will snap.'

TINA: *Training the horses does take a lot of Henrietta's attention, but it is not her only responsibility. A racehorse trainer is also a co-ordinator, and, rather like the director of a film, holds all the strands of the project together. Henrietta has had plenty of preparation in her life for this, firstly as one of the first official point-to-point trainers, training over a hundred winners, but perhaps most significantly as Chairman of the Selectors for the British Event Team. It was during her time in this role that Great Britain won the team silver medal at the Seoul Olympics.*

Dealing with people

'Training racehorses is not just about training them, it's about dealing with the owners, jockeys and everything else. You cannot train horses in isolation. You've got to think of the human aspect. If you can't handle people, you may as well not try training at all.

'As a selector, I learnt how to deal with horses and people under pressure, especially all the people – the owners, the grooms, the veterinary side and so on. Certainly at the Olympics there was a lot of pressure, and a lot of times when people tried to take you off course; but if you believe that what you are doing is right, you must stick to that belief and not be side-tracked. You can listen to other people, that's fine, but not have the whole pattern you are following changed by too many people's opinions.

'I'm much better under pressure; I need it for the best to come out. I was always better at school when I was doing exams, I can get a bit casual in the everyday world. But when the pressure is on and you have a real deadline, some people react worse, some better. Often when you are training for a big race or competition, people start panicking and bring up things they've never brought up before.'

> **TINA:** Nowhere is this policy of sticking to one's principles tested more than in Henrietta's production of Best Mate. She follows a strict regime of only running him three times before his big race, the Cheltenham Gold Cup. She meticulously picks the preparation runs that she thinks will suit him best, paying close attention to the course conditions and his opponents.
>
> Arguments rage in the press, in racing chat rooms on the web, and probably in the bars of every racecourse in Great Britain, about whether she is right or wrong. The doom mongers see it as a failure of training when he might have an off day, such as at Leopardstown where he ran second to Beef or Salmon, a horse he had easily beaten before. This is despite the fact he had injured his head on the way over to Ireland, and then was found to be coughing the next day, a more than adequate explanation for his below-par performance. However, in a world where so many 'experts' freely expound their often misinformed opinions, it would be easy, in a moment of doubt, to be swayed.

Keeping things in perspective

'It is very important to keep things in perspective, and I don't worry too much what the public think. When I was training to be a teacher, I remember one of our lecturers telling us: "Don't go into the classroom and set out to be liked: go in there and set out to do what you think is right. And if you do that, you will get respect, and then you'll be liked. If you try to be liked, you'll probably end up making a fool of yourself, and people won't like you anyway."

'With the training of horses, I do what I think is right, I take my own line and I stick to it, and I tend to disregard what the press and everyone else says. If we read everything they wrote about Best Mate, we'd go mental. Because the horse has got to the top, it is like being a top sportsman: he's there to be shot at. I remember when Steve Davis, the snooker player, won everything. People got bored of him and started knocking him, and moved on to supporting the next up-and-coming player. It's human nature, especially in the English. Everyone at the top is there to be shot at, and everyone has their own opinion. Luckily, I can shut off to all that, although I do get desperately worried inside beforehand about a race going right.'

> TINA: *Although she does not have to read the papers, it is impossible to completely avoid the public glare, and Henrietta is constantly called upon to comment on how her horses are, or how she feels they ran in a race. She is often remarkably candid in her comments and what she reveals.*

Honesty is the best policy

'If you start telling lies, it's amazing how it gets found out, especially when you've got a big yard, and lots of staff, who go to the pubs and meet people from other racing yards. The things we hear about from other yards when the staff come back from a day's racing; you ask yourself, how could they know that?

'So I always tell the owners first what is going on so they know, then I tell other people. Obviously we don't tell everybody everything, but we don't tell lies.'

> TINA: *Henrietta's dedication is second to none. She and Terry get up at 5.30 every morning to feed all the horses, because, with the heavy schedule of racing and training, there are many days when this is the only chance she gets to check every horse close up.*

'There's no short cuts!'

'It's quite a wrench getting out of bed. That alarm goes just before five every morning, but you get used to it. In the middle of winter I leave around 9.15 most days to go to the races and don't get back till after dark, so I only get to see one lot out. This means the only time we see the horses is when we feed them in the morning.

'You've got to drive yourself, I mean sometimes I feel I drive myself almost to the point where I think if I was a horse I might crack up. But if you are doing anything that's worth doing, you've got to put in the hard work -- and as your father would say, "There's no short bloody cuts!" If you are doing something, you need to be single-minded, and drive yourself and keep motivated. There are times, though, when I nearly collapse from exhaustion.

'You've always got to have a goal. When I started, my goal was to have a runner in the Gold Cup. Now we have won three, we would like to see if we can find another horse that is capable of running in, or even winning another Gold Cup. We probably will never get another like Best Mate, but you never know, we could get another good one.'

TINA: *This last sentence, I feel, reveals a little of Henrietta's superstition. My father always believed that the best way to run a successful business was to start small and then steadily build it up. Those who started with something large and flashy usually could not cope with what they had, and the business would fall apart. This is what Henrietta has done with her whole life. From simple beginnings running a livery yard, to working with young horses, graduating to point-to-pointers, and then taking out a trainer's licence proper, Henrietta has put one solid brick on top of another. It is this depth of experience and strength of character that has helped her weather the storms of racing, and makes her one of the most thorough and skilful trainers in the country. And I, for one, believe there are a few more good winners to come out of West Lockinge yet.*

expert insight

'If you are doing anything that's worth doing, you've got to put in the hard work – and as your father would say, "There's no short bloody cuts!" You need to be single-minded, and drive yourself and keep motivated.'

Anne Kursinski:
Keeping It Simple

Anne Kursinski

Anne is a passionate and intuitive trainer who has instilled
style and horsemanship into thousands of American hunter
and jumper riders. An Olympian and prolific Grand Prix winner
in several continents over the last thirty years, she combines
flair with a simple yet profound approach to training both
horses and riders.

It is a pleasantly warm afternoon at the beginning of the Winter Equestrian Festival in Florida, and Anne Kursinski is helping a young professional rider on a chunky, yet free-jumping German horse.

'Eyes and hands, eyes and hands,' she calls out as the rider jumps around the course. The fences have been set out on a variety of related distances: an upright with three strides to a Swedish oxer, five strides on a slight curve to another parallel. Anne is reminding her student to keep her eyes up, always looking where she is going in order to maintain a consistent focus from fence to fence. The 'hands' part of the reminder is that she uses her hands as a pair to turn, rather than pulling on one rein. The instructions do not get any more complicated than that.

Anne has been one of the best known and most popular jumping coaches in North America for over twenty years. She has also been one of their most consistent and able competition riders, winning extensively in America and Europe – the Aachen and Rome Grand Prix, a member of the silver medal-winning team at the Seoul Olympics, team and individual gold medallist at the PanAm Games. More than that, she is a stylish and effective horsewoman, who promotes a strong sense of fair play for the horse. As Hoffy, her partner says, 'Anne's horses are the luckiest in the world, because it is never their fault.'

Anne was born in California, and her early mentor was the legendary Jimmy Williams, who she rode with from the age of eleven until she was twenty-five. Jimmy was an all-round, old-fashioned type of horseman, who trained most of the professional show jumpers on the West Coast, and who had every type of horse imaginable through his yard.

Getting the most out of a horse

'The horse fascinated Jimmy. He would talk about cowboy psychology, about getting inside the horses and being able to read a horse well. He trained Western horses, racehorses and saddlebreds. He had dabbled in dressage and jumping whilst he was in Italy during the Second World War. Many professionals came to him with all kinds of problem horses. By the time I got there, his main interest was hunters and jumpers, but he still worked on them from the standpoint of getting inside the horse in order to get them to do different things.

'He believed that to be a great horseman or woman, you should be able to do many different things, not just one thing. Could you get a horse to do one-time changes, or jump five feet, or slide like a Western horse? Today that is difficult because the quality of each discipline is so much better, and so to be a champion at anything you do have to specialize. But the idea of how to get the most out of each horse, or even helping a horse to change career from jumping to being a dressage horse, can still be very useful.

'Jimmy could get the horses to do all sorts of tricks, like lie down, or stand on their hind legs. A lot of people today don't have a clue how to do that sort of thing, so I am so grateful that I had that time. I might not do it just how he did it, often it was very strong, sometimes rough, perhaps not in the horse's best interests. But that was Jimmy's style, and to see how to get a horse to do anything was fascinating. For me as a child, to be told go jump that five foot six oxer, and I'd think, "I don't know what I'm doing, but here goes…" that sort of "Go do it" attitude was very good for me, although now I would do it with more knowledge and feeling.

'He also put me together with a saddlebred trainer, who got me a suit and I won a ladies' five-gaited class, so I learnt how to do that, too. Another professional had Lippizaner and high-school horses that were used in the movies, and I worked with him for some time. Jimmy was very good like that, sending me out in different directions, and it gave me yet another chance to say "How do I get inside this horse?"

'He was a very good teacher, but with me, probably because I was talented and I was good, it was always that I wouldn't be good enough, so I had to keep working at it. If I had a little success, he would right away put me on a horse that would rear or stop or fall down, so he showed me there was always more to learn.

'In a way that was a good thing, to make me an Olympian, because it made me always want to be better. He wasn't like that with all his students. Like training a horse, he was very good about each horse being different, so with the chicken rider, or the little girl that wasn't going to go too far, he would tell her how great she was, and it would make me nuts!

expert insight

'The idea of how to get the most out of each horse, or even helping a horse to change career from jumping to being a dressage horse, is very useful.'

'I rode thousands of horses with him. He was a dealer so we had good, bad, stopping, leg-hanging, winners, terrible horses, but that experience, along with the nice ones my mother also gave me to ride, is something you just can't get without putting your leg over a lot of horses.'

TINA: Jimmy also sent her off to work with dressage rider Hilda Gurney. Hilda was an incredible woman, whose life was reminiscent of the film International Velvet, winning a bronze medal in dressage at the Montreal Olympic Games, having paid her way there by working as a schoolteacher.

Hilda Gurney's influence

'Hilda would come out and teach classical dressage to me and the other professional girls at Jimmy's, every Tuesday night, for four or five years. I really stuck with that, and ended up showing at Grand Prix level and trained my own horse to Prix St Georges. She gave me a good classical understanding of getting the horse on the bit, riding them from the back to the front.

'She was a great influence, and I always made extra time to watch her work. This woman had no money, nothing. She didn't even really have the right physique to ride, but she did it, and went to the Olympics, and her story of how she got there was such an inspiration. She would tell me "Come on honey, you can do it!"

'It was a fantastic opportunity, to watch her and others around her like Klimke and Theoderescu, who would come and give clinics, and absorb this classical understanding of dressage. I would go and hang out at the clinics and meet them. I was a nobody, but I just wanted to be better.

'The time with Hilda was invaluable, and my flatwork still has a lot of her influence.'

TINA: Anne did become a very successful competitor on the West Coast in America, though she was, as she herself put it, 'a big fish in a small pond.' Various riders and trainers encouraged her to spread her wings, either to come to the much more competitive East Coast, or to go to Great Britain. In the end she settled on moving to George Morris's Hunterdon. George is probably the most influential show-jumping trainer in America: brilliant, outspoken and with an infinite capacity for attention to detail.

Going east

'In 1981, George Morris came to judge a show at Flintridge in California, and said to me, "You really ought to come east." Some of Jimmy's other riders had gone east before, to jump at the indoor shows or for selection trials, so I organized a tour, and joined up with George with some of Jimmy's horses.

'George was both similar to Jimmy, and at the same time also very different. I think I fitted in because I was a "good soldier", with a "Whatever you tell me to do, I'll do it" attitude. That was the way I was raised, and that was the way Jimmy demanded it to be, so that's what I knew, and that helped me fit in.

'George didn't try to change my style in a big way. He told me he wasn't going to "unteach" whatever I had, whatever Jimmy had taught me, and whatever I had naturally. Initially I had ridden a little different from his way: a little stiff, a little backward, and adding strides. This was due slightly to riding in rings in California. I hadn't really ridden out in fields because we did not have them, so to really let a horse gallop and jump was a bit different for me. George helped me ride more that way.

'He never admits to remembering this, but at that show he judged in California, where I think I won the Grand Prix, he told somebody that I was too old to change (twenty-two) and if I went east I wouldn't make it. Probably that pushed me on, because I heard he had said I couldn't do it, so by God, I was going to do it.

'So how I was ever courageous to leave that little world, where I was pretty successful, and go east, I don't know, but something inside said, "I want to be the best, I want to be the best," so I had to get out there and give it a try.'

> **TINA:** *This desire to always improve fuels Anne's teaching as well, but the mechanics of how to make 'being better' a reality are based on a very simple idea.*

Learning to be aware

'To me, riding is all about awareness. It is self-awareness, the control of your body, so you know where your heels or your hands or whatever are. Also your emotions, are you being aggressive, are you fearful, are you nervous at the horse show? I have taken this maxim of Dan Millman's, "To compete like you train, and train like you compete." This means that you are as focused and sharp when you are training as when you compete, and yet as relaxed in the ring as you are in training. So first you must have awareness of yourself, and then an awareness of the horse. Is he long-striding, short-striding, lame, is he crooked?'

> **TINA:** *As with the majority of trainers, Anne teaches that sound flatwork is the basis to successful jumping, because if you do not follow this premise, all problems that occur on the flat will be magnified when you come to jump.*

Influencing the horse

'The basics of your flatwork are that you must be able to get the horse to go forward, to come back, and turn left and right with the minimum amount of effort.

'What is also important is how you influence the horse. Can you consciously send him forwards, can you consciously slow him down? "Consciously" is the most important word here. I see riders half slowing the horse down, but the horse is still running away with them, and it is only ten strides later that they realize the horse is still accelerating.

'Ninety-nine per cent of the time when horses are not responding properly, not shortening enough, or not doing the shoulder-in properly, for instance, it's the rider's aids that aren't correct, or they are not being clear about what it is they want. Very often people make mistakes simply by being too vague, so the horse doesn't really know what the rider wants, and that's when trouble starts. You don't have to be abusive to say "This is what I want". It's not always about being strong, it's about being clear and focused. When you are like that, you can ride in a light way, but still be firm if the horse is green or confused.

'If you really stop and look, and if you come from the horse's perspective, he isn't co-operating because he's confused.'

> **TINA:** *When Anne approaches a training session, she does not come with a fixed idea of what she is going to work on. She prefers to 'feel' her way in and respond to how the horse and rider are on that particular day. However, she finds with most new students that the first thing she needs to pay attention to is their seat.*

expert insight

'Style is so important because it allows you to be in an effective position to communicate with the horse.'

The importance of style

'A secure position is so important. If you can't control your own body, how are you going to influence the horse properly? One lady I had recently, who had been showing (competing) somewhere else, I didn't allow to jump more than cross-rails for nearly a year because she was so dangerous-looking.

'I don't teach a good position to win equitation classes, although some of my riders really could win one of those classes, but to me, style is so important because it allows you to be in an effective position to communicate with the horse.'

> **TINA:** *The American show-jumping seat tends to be a little different from the European seat. Although many European riders move between a forward seat and sitting lightly in the saddle, the emphasis tends to be with the seat closer to the saddle. In the American style, where the horses often go in a much freer way, the rider is almost constantly out of the saddle, only becoming more upright in order to assist the horse in shortening in front of a fence, or to influence him to 'wait' in some way.*

The rider's seat

'The riders need to be able to get into a two-point position. I always teach the forward seat. Yes, they need to be able to do dressage and sit in the saddle so they can do collection, and yet when it is time to jump I was always taught to be in the two-point, with a secure lower leg.

'Another pet peeve of mine is the automatic release. I want the riders to jump with a straight line from their elbow to the horse's mouth. Most of the time in Europe riders release like that over the fence, but here a lot of people do the "crest release" (where the hand goes up the top of the neck) and you see photos of the horses looking really uncomfortable and trapped in their jowl. The "crest release" is useful for really novice riders, so they can grab the mane or use the neck for balance, but I train the automatic release, in order to test the rider's balance.

'One of my first exercises is to get the rider to turn their reins over so they hold them between their first finger and thumb and spread their hands wide, so they can follow the horse over the fence and prove they can keep their balance because of their position, not because of their hands. But if the rider is not secure in their lower leg, they are not going to be able to do that. You have to have that good firm base of support in the heels and the lower leg, then you can be with the horse.'

TINA: *Anne's attention to her rider's seat pervades all her training, not just those at a novice level. Working with the young professional, Holly Orlando, she spots that when the talented but slightly green horse she is sitting on needs correcting, Holly tends to pull on one rein, the right, which is also the direction the horse is running out to in front of the fence.*

Understanding why something happens

'Instead of doing the automatic release, Holly is stronger on the right. When she feels like she needs to get strong, instead of staying centred and using both reins, she goes directly to using the right rein. Again, this is just awareness. The horse is not bad when he runs out, although he will take advantage of her weakness. So it's not about beat the horse up because he ran out and pull it back to the left, but getting the riders to understand why something happens.

'You don't need to sit down and have a long dissertation about it: just see what happened because of this little habit the rider has.'

TINA: *A common problem I come up against is that when less experienced riders learn about flatwork, they can get involved with trying to keep the horse in a round shape when they go into the fence. If this is not done skilfully it takes the horse's concentration off the fence, which usually results in the horse jumping in a flat way. However, I saw a solution to this in the way Anne works. She is very keen to have the horses working in a round shape on the flat, that they be obedient off the aids, and move sideways with ease. Yet when it comes to jumping, in common with many American riders, she allows the horse to have his nose well in front of the vertical, and rides him with a very light hand, and the horse almost in a galloping type of stride. This is quite different to the more compressed way often seen in Europe.*

Letting the horse express himself

'Do your flatwork, and yet when it's time to jump, let go. It's not that you forget all of it: the horse must bend a little in the turns and be looking where he is going, making his flying changes and lengthening and shortening when you want, but the head down and on the bit – or as some Europeans have them, behind the bit – I don't think that is necessary.

'The flatwork is going to the gym, making him stronger and building the muscles of his topline, and if you do good work there the horse does not need

'The flatwork is going to the gym, making him stronger and building the muscles of his topline, and if you do good work there the horse does not need to jump so much. But when it's time to jump, get off his back and let him go.'

to jump so much. But when it's time to jump, get off his back and let him go.

'I think some of it comes from riding hot Thoroughbreds off the track in California. All you could do was follow them around, finesse them around the fences. The Europeans originally rode much heavier horses, which had to be ridden with a deeper seat and in a stronger style. Jimmy learned most of his jumping from the Italian school, the forward seat, which suits the hotter horses, and so that is what I was taught. Also I watched so many horses free jump, and they don't have anyone pulling their head down and making them bend and flex, they just get on and jump. You learn then that if you get out of their way, the horse can do it quite naturally.

'Also being a woman, not that I can't be strong, but I prefer being with the horse, not against him. I want to take what he can do and use it. After all, God taught him how to jump, so he knows more about it than we do. Then I can help his style with my position if I use it in the right way, perhaps sitting up a little to encourage him to steady in a combination, for instance.'

TINA: *The challenge is that less experienced riders tend to need a lot more jump training than the horses do.*

Helping body awareness

'The idea of being able to stay out of the horse's way, that is what is so difficult and takes a lot of practice: to accompany the horse, to allow the horse to express himself over the fence. Many times the riders take away the horse's jump, hitting it in the mouth or goosing it, not allowing it to jump like it could. The way I was raised, I don't overjump the horses. So in order to give the riders what they need, and keep the horses fresh, I school a lot over low fences.

'If they have another horse to practise on, then great, but then there is the mental part. I tell the riders that they have to figure it out, whether that's by using visualization, really thinking about the last lesson they had, or watching themselves on video. I also encourage people to go to the gym, because doing the different exercises can help your legs, help you balance. Now I didn't go to the gym before 1988 and I'd already ridden at two Olympic Games, so you don't have to go, but it can help, as can yoga, ta'i chi, anything that helps body awareness.'

TINA: *Anne does use trot and grid exercises to work on the rider and horse's style. However, she finds that as useful as these can be, they can also build up a false confidence if over-used. Therefore about 75 per cent of her jump training is done over related distances and courses, so the rider is well versed in the way they need to ride in the ring.*

The day I watched Anne working was typical of this. She had set up a course that could be jumped in various different directions, with related distances of three, four, five, six and seven strides, on straight lines and doglegs. After doing some straightforward flatwork to warm up, the riders started by jumping over a single filler without wings, about two feet high, on a figure of eight. Then she went straight on to jump the course, set at about 3ft 9in (1m 15cm). This was quite a big leap from what they had been jumping, but then these were riders who were used to riding with Anne, and the point of the lesson was that she wanted them to commit to a competition pace.

It takes a certain amount of courage to go into this stronger pace, but it is absolutely necessary to do so if the horse is to be able to cope with the related distances. The bigger fences make the riders commit to this pace: if she let these riders jump around 3ft 3in (1m), they could get away with being underpaced and would not learn this vital lesson.

Maintaining focus

'Normally I would go in smaller increments, but the horse show is coming up, and so these riders need practice in jumping over courses, and yet I don't want to jump the horses so much that they lose their enthusiasm.

'The biggest thing with the small obstacle was the straightness. This is, of course, a mental question. A narrow thing like that and the riders go into "Oh my God, he's going to run out" instead of staying focused and centred. Then with the course, again they need to have a good position and then really have a focus of what they want. If it's to move down four long strides or shorten up, or make a turn in a certain place, by God, no matter what the horse is doing, they need to stay in position and keep that focus.

expert insight

'If you can control your own body and have that focus, riding is not difficult. Some teachers go on and on and get very involved, but horses are very simple animals. It's the human beings that are complicated.'

'If you can control your own body and have that focus, riding is not difficult. Some teachers go on and on and get very involved, but horses are very simple animals. It's the human beings that are complicated.'

> **TINA:** *Maintaining this focus and catching riders on where they lose concentration is one of the main thrusts of Anne's teaching. She puts a lot of emphasis on encouraging the rider to always look where they are going, for where the eyes go, the mental concentration usually follows. Not only that, when the rider's focus is consistent, the horse latches on to it and responds accordingly.*

A telepathic influence

'I also believe that horses do "see" through our eyes. There is an energetic quality to it, so that when you are focused the horse feels where he is supposed to go, what he is supposed to do. If you are not right there, or your eyes are wandering about, the horse can be all over the place.'

> **TINA:** *The value of consistent focus cannot be over-estimated. What is even more effective is when the rider creates within themselves a sense of what they want the horse to feel like in a movement or in his working frame. By going inside and using your imagination in this way, you have the chance of that being reflected almost automatically on the outside. This is because the horse picks up on that energy and responds accordingly.*

Inspiring confidence

'I get on horses at clinics that have been naughty, and I put myself in a good position and become focused, and the horses nearly always get it. I got on one horse the other day and the rider said, "But you didn't really do anything!" I just got on, my back stayed relaxed and I just put this feeling over to the horse, "I know you can go round, put your head down and relax, I know you can do it."

'Pretty soon the horse does it. You don't need to bend and flex and pull at him. I could do a big show, and some trainers do, but I think that's about their ego. Anyone can pull a horse around, but I do believe it's deeper, not just hands and legs, and counting strides. To me it's the magic, the invisible part, that's the fascinating part. On some level, psychic or whatever you want to call it, there is this feeling of putting over what it is I want. And sometimes of course I need to leg-yield it a little, or touch the horse with my spur, but to get his attention only, not much more. It's a sense of "Okay buddy, I know you can do this" and the sense back from the horse is "Oh goodness, thank you."

'The horse can be resisting at first, but when you start to ride differently he will respond. The resistance is usually something a rider has trained into them by being antagonistic, or has been confused themselves and so has confused the horse, but then the horse will surrender when he feels this sense of understanding being put over to him. Occasionally you have a real donkey, but even those, nine times out of ten, unless they have a physical problem or have had a history of very bad treatment, they will get it, in a much lighter way.

'Linda Tellington Jones has a neat saying about this: "It's not you feeling the horse, it's you feeling the horse feel you back." In my teaching, it's not just about beating them up and saying you do it because I say you do. I want the horse to "get it". I want him to understand, and for that the rider has to sense the horse "getting it".'

TINA: *The passion that Anne still has to help riders and horses comes from a very deep place inside her – not just to ride well and compete and be better, but also to do the best for the horses.*

'The horses are my teachers'

'I so often say in my clinics, I'm not really here for you, I'm here for the horses. I am here as a mouthpiece for the horses. Your horse is trying to tell you this, maybe that he needs to see the vet, or his back is painful. If they are acting up, or knocking the fences down, or even when they are being perfect, they are trying to tell us something: "Get some more lessons", "Get a new saddle", "I don't want to jump this high", whatever it is. Very often by the end of the clinics

I thank the riders because they are my teachers. Thank you for demonstrating to me, because I might not quite know what I am going to say and I am experimenting with them to see what works, even to this day.'

TINA: *Despite her genuine love of teaching and passing on her knowledge, Anne is still also a competitor.*

The will to win

'I'm still competing because I still want to win. I'd love to go back to Aachen or the Olympic Games. There is nothing like riding with the best in the world on a horse that really can do it, although I wouldn't want to go if I did not have a good enough horse. But it's a personal thing. Recently I won a good class at Harrisburg, however the day before I really could have won this other class, but I went down a distance in eight strides instead of seven. So the challenge is always there to be better, to keep asking, can I do it? And how well can I do it? And it's not just the winning, but to do all the things I am teaching, all the things I say to my students.'

TINA: *As I watched Anne working with her students, and later when talking to her, a single phrase kept going through my mind: 'Simple awareness is often curative.' For these are the hallmarks of her work: simple instructions, a lot of patience, and constantly raising her students' awareness about what her horses are trying to communicate.*

For the love of the horse

'My biggest thing is always, the horses first. Are you standing them on their heads too much? Are you going to the well every time? We must never forget the

---

expert insight

'The challenge is always there to be better, to keep asking, can I do it? And how well can I do it? And it's not just the winning, but to do all the things I am teaching, all the things I say to my students.'

horse. Many people are making a nice living, enjoying themselves, but it mustn't be at the horse's expense. We all got into it for the animal, and we must never forget that. I am so proud that Eros, whom we have had since he was five, is still going at eighteen. I encourage my students the same way, talk to the blacksmith, talk to the veterinarian, I want you to know what is going on with the horses.

'For me, it's still the love of the horse. Olympics or no Olympics, it's still the horse, and hopefully you win a little too, but not at his expense.'

expert insight

'We must never forget the horse. Many people are making a nice living, enjoying themselves, but it mustn't be at the horse's expense. We all got into it for the animal, and we must never forget that.'

Kyra Kyrklund:
Working with What You've Got

Kyra Kyrkland

Former World Championship silver medallist and trainer of more than thirteen horses to Grand Prix level, Kyra is one of the world's most popular dressage trainers, leading clinics and symposiums all over the globe. Especially noted for her no-nonsense approach, she has influenced thousands of dressage riders to train with thoughtfulness, and, particular regard for the horse's psychology.

If you were a dressage fan in the late eighties and early nineties, you will remember the eye-catching combination of Kyra Kirklund and Matador. One of the first of the more modern type of dressage horse, he was a compact, black ball of energy, who lit up a dressage arena with his extravagant, powerful movement, winning the Hamburg Dressage Derby, the Volvo World Cup and a silver medal in the World Championships in Stockholm.

However, Matador was only one of more than thirteen horses that Kyra has both trained and ridden at Grand Prix level. She has also become a popular and sought-after trainer across the globe, as well as chief dressage trainer at Flyinge, the National Stud in Sweden, for several years.

One of the main reasons behind Kyra's success as both a rider and a trainer is her simple methodology. One friend of mine observed that, 'Not only is it clear what she is asking the horse to do, it is also perfectly obvious to those watching why she is doing it. If I can understand it from the floor, then surely the horse must understand it easily, too.' For Kyra, however, riding is not just about asking the horse to perform movements, but is part of something much bigger.

Riding, an approach to life

'Riding is a lot of philosophy, not only technical: it is an approach to life, much more than I thought at the beginning, and that's probably why you never learn fully because there are so many new angles that you can see.

'When you have problems in a movement, it is not the movement that is the problem, there is another cause of the problem. Okay, maybe it's a bit of a longer way, but it's definitely a better way to go back to the point where you can start to change, and then build up from there again.'

Kyra's philosophy of riding

At the heart of Kyra's philosophical approach is the desire for the horse to respond in an absolutely genuine way to the aids. This comes before putting it on the bit, or teaching it any specific movement. In practical terms this is known as Kyra's ABC, which consists of the three most basic signals that the horse must learn.

Firstly, the horse needs to respond to the lower leg by increasing his speed, otherwise known as the forward aid. Secondly, he should slow down or stop for a restraining hand on the rein. Finally there is the turning aid, a combination of weight, lower leg and rein, which influences the horse to go in the direction the rider wants.

Kyra uses her ABC to establish communication when she first gets on a horse, particularly a young one. She does this by asking the horse to halt with a quiet but definite hand closing around the rein. As soon as the horse stops, she releases the contact by giving the reins. This is a reward for the horse's right response, and it must be instantaneous so the horse hears, 'Yes! That is what I wanted.'

If the horse moves forwards before being asked to, she will stop him again, and then reward him by giving the rein.

At the same time as using this restraining hand, Kyra also takes care to stabilize her seat by closing her stomach muscles, so that she maintains her balance when the horse stops. This stabilizing of the seat will later become a weight aid that influences the horse to slow down or collect. If the horse learns at an early stage to associate slowing down with this weight aid, the hand aid can become correspondingly lighter.

When the horse stands still in a satisfactory way, Kyra then closes her lower leg. As soon as the horse responds to the leg, the leg pressure is released. Again this is the instantaneous reward: if you respond well, the aid ceases. The horse soon picks up on the fact that the sooner he responds, the sooner the aid is released. This means that the leg aid can also become a lighter and subtler one.

Kyra is also scrupulous about the quality of the response. If the horse is slow to respond, she will send him forwards with a stronger leg aid, and if that does not illicit a positive enough response, she uses the leg together with the voice or the whip behind the girth. If she needs to do this she will expect the horse to shoot forwards and canter off briskly. She is then ultra-careful to let the horse go forwards with complete freedom from the hand, making sure that she is in balance and does not bump on the saddle in any way. After all, when the horse has finally given a truly positive response, the last thing the rider must do is unwittingly 'punish' him by causing him pain in the mouth or the back.

This basic work is based on an understanding of the way the horse functions physically. A horse cannot carry himself well if his engine – that is, his hind-quarters – is not engaged, just like you need to put a car into gear and press the accelerator to get it to move forwards. By making sure she gets a clean response when she presses her 'accelerator', Kyra creates the situation where the horse will find it easy to carry himself in the way she wants.

Once the horse has understood the first two aids, Kyra starts to combine them into the turning aids. When she does this, many horses come into a good working shape of their own accord.

Why put so much emphasis on the response to these basic aids? Because if the horse is not giving a truly genuine response to them, all the other work that the rider does is going to be compromised. This is why, when she has a problem with a horse, even an experienced one, Kyra will return to this routine to make sure the basics are in place.

Influencing the horse

'When you really want to influence the horse then you put him between your aids, and use them all together. Suddenly though, you find that you are using too much leg, or too much hand, so if I get into a situation like this, I separate the aids up by going back to the ABC. It's so easy that you start to lie to yourself, and this is a good way to find out the truth of what is happening.'

> TINA: This work to make sure that the horse responds truly to the aids comes before putting the horse on the bit. For in Kyra's experience, when the horse is submissive to these aids, the result will be that he comes into a soft working shape.
>
> This is in contrast to some other trainers who try to ask the horse to submit by putting the horse on the bit. This often results in the horse looking cosmetically correct, but with varying degrees of tension in his body. Using Kyra's method, the horse comes into shape willingly, because it is a natural progression from the work he has just done.
>
> In an ideal world, the horse carries himself in this shape with his poll at the highest point of the curve of his neck, and his nose just in front of the vertical. However, Kyra is happy to allow the horse to be slightly in front of, or behind the vertical when he is doing a movement in training, if he is more comfortable that way, so that he learns to carry out the movements with ease.

The feeling of being in balance

'There are so many different ways of being on the bit. There is one visual aspect that you present to the judges, but then there is another, which is a feeling, of the horse being in a good balance, and being really true.'

> TINA: When a horse is first learning a movement, Kyra doesn't mind if the horse corners off the bit, as long as he responds to her aids and carries out the movement.

expert insight

'When you teach the horse something new, you are going to upset their balance. It's more important that the horse learns to do a movement and when he technically knows what he is going to do, then he can go on the bit.'

Finding his own balance

'When you teach the horse something new, you are going to upset their balance, so you can't ask him to be in perfect balance. For instance, you unbalance him when you teach him the flying change. For me, it's more important that the horse learns to do the flying change and then he can go on the bit, when he technically knows what he is going to do and he starts to find his own balance. But if the rider just wants the horse to stay in the right outline, then you hinder him from doing things.'

TINA: *Kyra has a great understanding for the horse's mental make-up. For example, when she is teaching a horse a new movement, she tends to ask the horse to go in a slower tempo whilst he is learning that movement. Being a 'flight' animal, a horse's natural tendency is to flee from any situation he finds difficult or threatening. That is why a horse will often tend to go faster when you ask him something he does not understand. By slowing the horse down, and by breaking the movement down into simple components, she gives him a chance to figure out what he is being asked. Of course, as soon as the horse responds, the aid is released and the horse rewarded.*

Despite having high ideals, Kyra is also a realist, and factors some degree of compromise into her training, according to a horse's strengths and weaknesses.

Riding to your horse's capability

'Teaching them something new, you might have to use your leg a bit more, or accept a bit more in your hand, just for that time whilst they are learning; but then you have to purify it again (that the horse is light in the hand and responsive to a light leg and weight aid) so you can go one step more.

'Then when you are in a dressage test, you need to realize that the judges might give you a six for a movement, but six for that horse is like ten for another horse. All horses have difficulties somewhere, and you can't just nag them about those problems. You can still win even if you have one movement that you only get a six for – as long as you don't get a two, or you ruin a lot of good things that are there by over-concentrating on the horse's weaknesses in their training. This is where I will compromise: if I feel the horse is doing the best he can do, of course I try to push for more at some stage; but then if I feel that this horse can't do any more, then I accept it and I let him be mentally happy with that.

'This is where dressage is different from show jumping: if you have a horse that always jumps into the water, then you have a big problem, and that problem you have to get over. But in dressage, if they dip a leg in one movement it doesn't matter so much, because it will only affect that movement.'

> **TINA:** However, Kyra is uncompromising in her attitude to the rider's seat. She emphasizes that when the horse is not doing what the rider wants it to, you must go to the root of the problem, and that root often lies in the rider's seat. For instance, a horse may go crooked, but when you pay close attention to the rider, you will see that they are actually 'collapsing' on one side and putting more weight on one seat bone.
>
> She also feels that there are two types of seat that a rider needs to learn. First that they can sit passively, where they learn to sit in a balanced way whilst absorbing the movement of the horse. Then, that they learn 'active sitting', where they learn to use their body and weight to influence the horse in a positive way.
>
> Kyra also recognizes that when a pupil is first learning something, part of the challenge can be that they don't actually know what they are looking for.

Learning by Demonstration

'When a student has problems, I get on the horse myself because that helped me when I went to Herbert Rehbein. He would get on the horse, and I could see that it could do better, and that inspired me to say it's not the horse – it can do better if I can ride him better. Now when I have trouble with a horse, I "see" Herbert on it and what it might do with him.' He was amazing.

> **TINA:** Getting on the horse not only gives the rider a visual idea of what they are looking for, it also enables Kyra to put the right feeling into the horse. Then when the rider gets back on, they get a chance to experience what it should feel like. Once a rider has experienced the right feeling a few times, it becomes much easier for them to create it themselves because they have a reference of what it is they are looking for.

Learning by feeling

'I think people are very different in the ways they learn, whether it's by seeing or reading or feeling. I try to find the way that is easiest for that person. I rely a lot on my feeling, but I try to understand people who can't because they don't have the same feeling. I do this by talking to them. I have one rider who is riding at Grand Prix, and he told me I need to tell him that this is the feeling he should go for, because he is not that secure that it is the right feeling.'

> TINA: *However good a trainer is, there are times when, just as a rider does not 'click' with a horse, a rider does not click with a trainer, or grows apart from them.*

Moving on

'I have learnt to accept that it is not that I am a bad teacher, or that the student is a bad student if it doesn't work, or we don't quite match. It is better then to move on to someone else, and neither I nor the rider needs to feel bad about that. I have learnt from a lot of different people anyway.

'When I had my training stable in Finland, George Morris would come sometimes, and because I had some students that I felt wanted to go, or it wasn't working that well with, I asked him what he did when he had students like that – and he said "Let them go. You can force them to stay for a year or two more, but they will never come back. It's better to send them out earlier, and then they will come back to you." And that is exactly what happened.'

> TINA: *Kyra has an innate ability to accept a situation as it is and respond accordingly. As a young rider in Finland, she competed in dressage, eventing and show jumping, and won at national level in all three, jumping in classes up to 1.50m. However, there came a point when she needed to choose one avenue.*

From jumping to dressage

'First of all, in jumping you do need to have more horses. Then I was working at a farm where they were importing Irish hunters that were supposed to be re-schooled to be jumping horses. A couple of them were real lunatics and one day, the man who had sold the horses, asked me to jump one of them, a very hot mare who was not very careful. He built an oxer at 1.40 out of elephant poles, and told me to give the reins in front of it and kick on. I was idiot enough to do it and I had a really bad fall.

'That was the beginning of me getting afraid of jumping. It took half a year before I admitted it to myself, and then it was easy. I had been doing dressage all the time anyway, and looking back, I always had better results in dressage. I was happy that I had done the jumping, and until a couple of years ago I still jumped a bit. I would have loved to do it, but I wasn't good enough or brave enough.

'Then, I think I would have changed anyway, because of the second horse I bought as a four-year-old. He definitely was not a jumping horse but he did go to Grand Prix, and I went to the Moscow Olympics with him, and I certainly wouldn't have got there with him in the show jumping!'

TINA: *Kyra takes the same pragmatic approach to her competing.*

Do your best on the day

'Competition riding is a different ball game from teaching and training. When you train you train over a longer period, and maybe every second week you have one day when you say, "Wow, this is it!" But for that "wow" moment to happen at the right time, at a competition when you are going to go in, is very unlikely. Many of the tests you do, you survive to a certain extent.

'A lot of riders may have been training well at home, but when they come to the competition the horse is a bit tense and they lose it themselves because the horse is not as good as he could have been. What has helped me over the years is not to compete against the others, but to compete against myself and my horse. I want to do as well on the day as we can.

'You can only change things that you can influence. I can't influence the judges, and I can't influence the circumstances at the show, I can only accept it and go with it and do the best I can on that day. You learn this the hard way. In Seoul, I really had a chance of a medal, and I was going for a gold medal, not a bronze or even doing a good show, and I didn't get any medal at all.

'But without that experience, I would never have won silver in the World Championships in Stockholm, because there I realized that the others can have a good day or a bad day, but I can't influence that either. I can only go there and do my best. Trying to beat the others only frustrated me anyway, because when you ride against the world's best names, and you know you won't beat them, you always feel unsatisfied, even if you knew your horse wasn't as talented.'

'If you have a horse that is not so elastic and you still push for the same sort of expression, then it can easily go to tension because the horse is overfaced. I would like to see that tension penalized more.'

TINA: *Even if you are not riding the most talented horse in the world, there are still ways that you can pick up decent scores, especially by riding your test efficiently and accurately, and seeing places in the test where you can pick up extra points.*

Riding a test accurately

'If you read any test carefully, you can see where to pick up easier points. In the Grand Prix for instance, one of the transitions from canter to trot is worth as much as the two times, or a piaffe. There are a lot of details where the good riders don't throw points away. At the end of the day, dressage is mathematics. You count the points together, and the one who has the most points, wins.

TINA: *Dressage will always be subjective, and Kyra would like to see horses judged more on their own merit, rather than against each other, in order to prevent lesser talented horses being pushed beyond their capabilities and caused unnecessary stress.*

Respect your horse's limitations

'Medium-good horses should not be pushed too far, more than they can give. A really good horse is so elastic that they are bound to look extravagant, but if you have a horse that is not so elastic and you still push for the same sort of expression, then it can easily go to tension because the horse is overfaced. I would like to see that tension penalized more, so that riders realized the limit of what that horse is capable of. I see a lot of frustrated horses in that way.'

TINA: *Kyra ends her book* Dressage with Kyra *in a courageous way. There is a photograph of her on a horse where things are clearly not going to plan. She writes of how most books are written describing the ideal horse and how to ride him...a horse that does not actually exist. In her typically modest way she suggests that hers is not* the only way, and that her intention is to share some of the keys that have worked for her over the years. It is, however, in my experience, one of the clearest and most deeply thought-out books I have ever read, so I asked her if she intended to write more.

In a nutshell

'We did work hard on it, and in a nutshell, that is what I wanted to say. There are more things that I have learnt and I could do a follow-up, but I would not change it, because it is what I believe in. You can never cover everything in a book or a video, but I tried to put down the most important things that I have learnt. If you get too technical, nobody will understand it.

'Writing a book makes you read and re-read what you have written because so many things can be misunderstood. Most theory books are trying to describe a feeling and that is almost impossible. A lot of things I have read before and I go back to, I suddenly see another meaning in it, and I can see that maybe the writer wanted that, but you can't translate it if you haven't experienced it.'

TINA: For Kyra as well, learning and education is an ongoing process.

Solving problems

'It is a common misconception that top riders don't have problems with their horses too, but we do, it's just you get better at solving them. Horses are not machines, you can give good aids with the right timing, but if the horse is not listening, or he is not responsive or he is not prepared to work together with you, it won't happen anyway. Less experienced people often think that if they get the right hand and the left leg just there, it will work, but it doesn't.

'Also, you can do the right thing, but you may have to do it ten times before the horse says, "Hmm, she doesn't change, maybe I have to change."'

TINA: For me, Kyra's greatest strength is her ability to balance clear ideals and to work with them in a less-than-perfect world. When I asked her about a horse that might find it difficult to go on the bit because it was thick through the jowl area, her answer was 'Send it show jumping!' Working with this practical approach has made Kyra one of the finest and most prolific dressage trainers in the world, accepting that although not everyone or every horse can be an Olympic champion, everyone can aim to reach the top of their ability.

David O'Connor and the Language of Horses

David O'Connor

Former Olympic Champion and Badminton winner, and currently head of the USEF, David has had a profound influence over the sport of horse trials in the USA not only through his competitive exploits, but also as a trainer and because of his involvement with the development of the sport in an organizational capacity. He trains horses by giving them 'puzzles to solve' and is deeply interested in the relationship between horse and human being, and how best to make that relationship a productive one.

David and Karen O'Connor have only been at their new property in Ocala for a couple of weeks, but it is already starting to look like home. There are horses in the paddocks, koi carp in the fishpond, newly erected stables in the barns. For the past ten years they have been based in Virginia, but having survived four winters so harsh that sometimes they could not get the horses out of their stables for weeks at a time, they decided, like many American riders, to have a winter base in the more civil climate of Florida.

When I arrive, David has just finished a lesson, and is about to work with a homebred four-year-old that he got on for the first time last week. My timing is excellent, because David is one of the few international competitors consciously to incorporate natural horsemanship techniques into his training, and now I am going to see him at work.

'Beanpole' is a good-looking grey gelding, by a thoroughbred stallion out of an Intermediate event mare that Karen used to ride. David takes him into a round pen, and lets him loose. The horse has an effortless swing to his trot, and a confident expression on his face. David indicates to the horse when he wants him to change direction by dropping his shoulder: the horse turns in and looks at him, and David sends him in the other direction.

He puts a pole out for the horse, and when he has trotted over that in an uncomplicated way, David turns it into a small fence. This is the first time the horse has left the ground, but he jumps in an easy round shape and with a neat technique.

David strokes all over his back with a stick, and then saddles him up. The horse stands quietly throughout, attentive to David, but relaxed. David puts on a Western halter, the type designed to put pressure on the poll and various places on the horse's head. He asks the horse to bend left and right. Then he jumps on his back and heads out to a ten-acre field, still in only a halter with reins made out of a long rope.

But this is not reckless, or an act of bravado. David can do this because he has introduced the horse to each stage of his work in logical increments. He never moves on until the horse has accepted the last stage.

Out in the field, Beanpole trots around the perimeter quite happily. David then makes a figure-of-eight in the middle, which he repeats a couple of times. Finally, the horse is asked to stop and back up. He has not been foot perfect; at first he hangs a little by the entrance to the field, but it is a minor wobble, and before we forget, a week ago this horse had never been sat on. Now he can be ridden around a large field in a halter.

He will continue to be ridden like this, before being introduced to a bit, for two to three months. David believes if you can teach the horse to turn and stop without it, then the introduction of the bit is something that can occur without fuss. He feels that asking the horse to deal with a foreign thing such as a bit, in connection with the first times they are taught to turn and stop, causes the horse to associate discomfort with those early ridden experiences.

David has been one of the leading lights in horse trials during the last fifteen years, and has won nearly every major title: Badminton, an Olympic gold medal, Kentucky, and a host of two- and three-star three-day events. Together with Karen, nine-times leading lady rider in the United States, they have become America's golden couple of eventing. Now, although he still has two Advanced horses, he has turned his focus more to bringing on young horses, running training camps for enthusiastic young event riders, and being head of the United States Equestrian Federation. But right from the beginning, communion with the horse has always been the most important consideration for him.

Making a life with horses

'It was the time alone with the horses that really hooked me in. Being around them, in the quiet times, especially as there was a lot of discord in my family. I still find that those times with the horses are the best ones.

'I never really thought I would be able to make anything of it, though. It wasn't until I went away for three-quarters of a year after high school that I found out how much I missed the horses, and I started looking into ways to be able to have a go and make a life with them. At the same time, the developing rider thing happened. If you were a young rider at a competition you would be automatically aware of Jack [le Goff] being at the competitions, watching you. At that time you did not apply to get on the scheme, you were just written a letter out of the blue, and that was a big deal.'

> **TINA:** *Jack le Goff was the first of two major influences on David, and the developing rider scheme was one where talented young riders were taken under his wing at the USET training headquarters at Gladstone, some of whom even based*

themselves there permanently. A powerful and strong-minded man, he ruled the roost of American eventing in the sixties and seventies, and under his sway, the American team had many international wins.

It was under his influence that David had many of his early successes — a silver medal at the Alternative World Championships at Bialy Bor in 1986 amongst them — but like many riders of that period, David found something lacking in the American scene. Not only were Advanced competitions few and far between, but the cross-country courses were not strong enough to provide the type of mileage necessary for riders to compete on equal terms with the best in the world. In addition, there was a narrow focus in American eventing that did not help the sport develop as a whole.

A move to the UK

'Karen and I left the States for a while because there was something about the British outlook that was not present here at that time. It was a sense of sportsmanship, doing the sport for the sport's sake. At that time, everyone who was competing in the United States was trying to get to the Olympics. Now over here, you have the sport for the sport's sake as well, not just trying to get on the team. To me, this is a much healthier environment.'

TINA: David nearly did not stay in Great Britain. He had brought Wilton Fair over to Badminton in 1991, but had a disastrous cross-country round, where Wilton Fair ran away, taking chancy stand-offs and eventually falling. David received some harsh criticism for this performance, and was about to fly his horses home when a meeting with my father changed his plans. He believed that the problems David was encountering were not as deep-rooted as some others thought, and with a few minor adjustments in training, David and Wilton Fair would be back on track.

So in 1991, David came to live at Waterstock, and my father instituted a change of attitude in the training of Wilton Fair (or 'Wilbur'). In my father's opinion, David was an excellent rider, he had just put too much pressure on the horse in his desire to get the best performance out of him. This had produced a lot of anxiety in the horse, which caused him to run away. Wilbur was therefore allowed to hack around a few competitions without any domination, so he lost that desire to run away. David then returned to serious competition with a different look to his riding, being placed in the British National Championships at Gatcombe, and a few weeks later, coming thirteenth at Burghley. David stayed on over the winter at Waterstock, and the following spring, came seventh at Badminton.

Learning from the Western world

'Jack taught me the technique of riding and how to compete. Lars was the first one who brought more of the thought process of the horse back into it. He was the one who put it all together for me. Then at the same time I found out about stuff that was happening in the Western world, and I thought there was tremendous possibility for its application to my riding and training. So I experimented away in the round pen at Waterstock. Everyone thought I learnt this natural horsemanship stuff in America, but it started in your round pen. For four years, I took every horse I could find, put them in that pen, and taught myself how to do it. Then I found out that there was a whole movement going on. I had absolutely no idea about that.

'I think there are tremendous things to be learnt from the Western world, particularly when applying it to young horses and troubled horses. The problem in the United States is that there is such a circus surrounding it, and the natural horsemen get really cult-ish about what they are doing. Unfortunately then the professionals write it off, and they miss what is valuable in the work. One of my goals in my life is to help bridge the gap.

'Actually, I found that we were much closer in our thinking than some of the natural horsemen thought we were. We want to create the same "look" in the horse, that he is solving the problem in front of him. The difference is that, for instance, I want my horse to jump the chair that's in front of him. But a natural horseman might want the horse to stand on the chair, and they think everyone should get their horse to stand on the chair. Instead though, I take the piece from their work that creates the "look" in the horse, and then go and use it for what I want. It's just about learning the language of horses.'

TINA: *When David talks about the 'look', he is referring to the attitude the horse displays, when he is inquisitive about what he is doing. If the horse is too concerned*

---

expert insight

'I think there are tremendous things to be learnt from the Western world, particularly when applying it to young or troubled horses. Unfortunately the professionals write it off, and they miss what is valuable in the work.'

with the human being, then it does not use its natural curiosity to solve the puzzle in front of it. David uses the parts of natural horsemanship that create a relationship between him and the horse so the horse trusts him, and whatever he asks the horse to do, thereby freeing him up to stay curious.

The quality of the horse's paces

'We don't want the whole deal; we just want some of the pieces. The biggest difference is that we work much more on the quality of the horse's paces. The natural horsemen look at the horse's response. They want the horse to do things with enthusiasm, as we do, but you need different techniques to improve the quality of the horse's paces.'

> **TINA:** This was self-evident in the lesson David gave after he had worked with Beanpole. This was with a rider and horse combination whose dressage marks were poor. The horse was stiff in the mouth, one-sided, and unwilling to go forwards. Here, David worked much more on the horse's response to the leg, not to use more and more leg as had been used on the horse in the past, and which he had learnt to ignore, but with a little bump with the leg or touch with the spur. David explained that the horse must learn to respond to the leg, and then that his reward was the release of the leg aid.
>
> As David rode the horse, consistently using his legs and releasing as soon as he got a response, the horse started to move forwards more of his own volition. He also started to soften in his mouth to the consistent contact David was giving him. The principle was the same, in that as soon as the horse gave, David gave. It was important, David commented, to view the stiffness in the horse's mouth as an effect, rather than a cause of the problem: thus fiddling away with the horse's mouth was not going to make him softer. Getting his body moving and more flexible would make him softer in the body, and the natural by-product would be a more relaxed mouth.
>
> To get the horse's body moving, he made changes of pace, and asked the horse to cross his hindlegs for three or four steps at a time in walk and trot. Working in this athletic way loosened up the horse, so he felt freer in his body and more willing to go forwards.'

How much leg?

'There is a lot of misunderstanding around the use of the leg. Bill Steinkraus was the first one I ever heard say anything about it. When somebody asked how much leg he used, he replied "Well, I never lied to him [the horse]."

He meant that if he put his leg on, it meant there was something serious ahead, jumpwise. I didn't understand this for years, but now I understand a lot more. If the horse is in a good balance, he can go down a line of fences by himself; then when you do need to influence him, what you do is going to get a response.

'This rider today was a classical example of someone who has been told you've got to drive the horse up together with your leg into your hand. So he's done it more and more, and the horse has gotten dead to the aids.'

TINA: *David had finished teaching now – not, incidentally, in an arena, but in the same large field that he had ridden the young horse in. He has always preferred to school the horses on grass, without the restriction of walls, firstly so he can use natural gradients to his advantage – asking the horse to lengthen his stride uphill for instance, to encourage more elevation, but also to make himself and his pupils consistently ride the line of their choice. It is so easy for a rider to be fooled in an enclosed arena that they are the one choosing their line, but it is only when you get out in the middle of a field that you find out if you or the horse are the one making the decisions.*

But the day is not over for David. There are horses in temporary accommodation, waiting for doors to be hung on their stables, and so we go into one of the new barns, David picks up his hammer, and we continue talking. On his mission to understand and learn better ways to train his horses, David has also developed his approach to jump training, especially through loose jumping the horses in the round pen.

The benefit of loose jumping

'Loose jumping has helped all our horses. I believe that part of our success in the last few years is because I have jumped the horses so much in the round pen. Even the Advanced horses, like Shannon and Giltedge, would go back in there every time their show jumping went a bit off. There is tremendous benefit for the horse to do it, but there is also great benefit for the rider to see how that horse really wants to jump. You can see how he solves the problem. Then when you get on, and you are going to hopefully help with the situation, you can help him in a way that is really going to make a difference.

'As you could see with the horse today, five days ridden away and the first time he jumps, his focus was completely on the fence, studying what he was doing. How can that not help you when you are going cross-country?

'Loose jumping has replaced a lot of the repetitive gymnastic jumping that we used to do, because I have found that when the horses jump on their own, we don't tend to have the rushing problems. Our gymnastics have also changed, so that we do a lot less trot gymnastics, and more canter exercises.'

TINA: *David also has his own particular ways of preparing himself mentally for a competition. Top-class athletes often talk about getting into the 'zone' in order to perform at their best, and David has found some personal ways to get himself into that optimum mental state.*

Focusing the concentration

'I've always been a person who's tended to get a little quieter at competition time. I like to be by myself in order to focus my thoughts. When I was younger I needed quite a lot of time to do that – now that on/off switch works a lot quicker. So when I am getting dressed I put some music on, often with a pair of headphones, so I cut out the world and move into a quieter zone. It's partly to cut out distraction, but it also allows me to see all the other things on the outside that might affect my performance much quicker. You have to get a bit calmer and quieter in your brain so you can see that sort of thing. Then you might have to adjust it, because if you get into too much of a tunnel, you end up not seeing something that can affect your performance. I see as many people making this mistake, of narrowing their focus too much, as ones that don't concentrate enough. They don't see what the thing is that the horse is actually reacting to.

'I also always do the last cross-country walk on my own, very early in the morning, because I want to focus in on my performance and not be distracted by others' opinions.'

TINA: *It is always a challenge to conjure a good performance out of a horse at the optimum moment, but even more so in the dressage at a three-day event with a very fit animal. David is a master at this, and it is little to do with physical practice, and everything to do with keeping the horse happy, confident and calm.*

Keeping the horse mentally relaxed

'It's not about wearing them down with lots and lots of work, but getting them to think about very simple things that they can do. We do a lot of what we call pattern work or impulsive exercises. There is the "Swedish castle",

'I see as many people making the mistake of narrowing their focus too much, as ones that don't concentrate enough. They don't see what the horse is actually reacting to.'

which I learnt at Waterstock. Then another like that, called the "four corners", where you make a 10m circle in each corner. Then we have the "in and out", which entails halting or a downward transition as you go into the corner of the dressage arena, and as you come out of it, so the horse is mentally waiting in those areas. Once you get to the competition, you have already trained all the movements, so the emphasis now is on mentally preparing them.

'I believe this is one of my biggest strengths, because when everyone else is trying to get the extra two or three per cent in the warm-up, my horses are mentally right, so if I need to amplify their movement, I can just do it. I am also not afraid of taking that chance, of knowing I have put the work in before so the horse can produce it on the day. I used to drive your father crazy by turning up at the last moment for a test, but it was especially good with a headshaker like Wilton Fair. I only needed seven minutes. I did not need hours and hours just before the test. Of course I had taken him out and worked him earlier in the morning, it was just part of the plan to bring him down as late as possible, to keep him mentally relaxed before the test.'

TINA: *Taking the horse in and out of the stable two or three times for short periods of work is a very useful way to lower their adrenalin, because after a while the horse realizes that nothing pressured is going to happen, and that becomes their mindset for the test.*

'They just go out there and do something they know they can do, and then go back in, happy.'

TINA: *One of David's greatest strengths is his ability to pull a triumph out of a disaster. In 1987, flying home after Border Raider had jumped into the ditch at Centaur's Leap at Burghley, David ended up sitting next to a man called David Lenaburg and explaining what sort of horses he would need to be an Olympic team member. David Lenaburg became one of David's most loyal and longstanding owners.*

Learning from experience

'I always think that things happen for a reason, so in the real down times when you are struggling, you get a gift like David. Likewise, I won the Olympics because of Blenheim the year before. I rode a horse that had changed, and I didn't realize it. Previously he had been eliminated at the World Championships at a Liverpool in the show jumping; at Blenheim there were three Liverpools and I over-rode them, and he had every line down. I had a three-rail lead, and lost the competition!

'But I have no doubt that that helped me win a gold medal the next year, because I went back to exercises I had learnt from Luis Alvarez Cevera whilst I was at Waterstock, to rectify the way I was riding related distances.'

TINA: *Now pouring his experience into training young horses and riders, David has strong views about the way for people to learn riding and horsemanship.*

The way forwards

'Apprentice yourself with someone you like. You have to have a solid foundation, built by a mentor. Then you can experiment from there, and learn about different ways, and bring all of those pieces back into your solid foundation. That is the key to anyone who wants to ride well. At the moment, people change around so quick, early on, so they don't get the solid foundation which they need in order to discern which pieces from other sports will be useful to them.

'Like with our natural horsemanship, Western ideas, we never wanted the whole thing. We were never going to flip over and turn into cowboys. I said, I like that piece, and that piece, and I'll take those into my thought process.

'The same when I go show jumping. I'll take those four pieces from that person, and integrate them into my philosophy. I had such a huge solid foundation built by your father and Jack, that's the way it worked for me. Yes, it's riding lots of different horses and disciplines, but there has to be a single thought process that runs through that, otherwise the person is just fishing.'

TINA: *He also has a simple philosophy about winning competitions:*

'Competition is only about the pursuit of excellence and if you pursue that all the time, and you're excellent at what you do, you'll win. At the moment,

> 'Apprentice yourself with someone you like. You have to have a solid foundation, built by a mentor.'

people learn to compete before they learn how to ride, and they learn how to ride before they learn the language of horses, and what you really want to do is back this process up. Learn the language, which may take different lengths of time for different people, learn how to ride, and then learn how to compete.

'That's our big thing, to learn the language of horses. Just like in writing, you need to learn letters, then words, then sentences, then paragraphs, and then you write your story, whatever you want to be. Whether it's in show jumping, or eventing, or natural horsemanship.

'We all started with ABCs. Edgar Allan Poe learnt classical literature first before he experimented with the English language and how to put it together. Now everyone wants to be a poet, but no one wants to learn their ABCs.'

TINA: *David, as head of the American Equestrian Federation, and working with the FEI, has a lot of say in the direction that three-day eventing is going in, and I wondered what he felt about the future.*

Breaking down the barriers

'We need to get some consistency in our sport right now. Its been through so many changes and ups and downs in the last four years that it needs to take a breath and stay on a course. What we have decided here in the United States is to keep our one- and two-stars as a full three-day event with the steeplechase, because we believe that it is an essential part of the educational process, although the higher-level three-days are going to be without the 'chase. We believe that the process of doing full three-day events at the lower levels educates future Olympic and younger riders. It also fits the needs of the amateur riders who want to have that as a goal. On a rainy day, when the ground churns up, an event that doesn't have a steeplechase still turns into an endurance test, and we want riders to be educated for that. It will help them be more rounded horsemen.

'However, in horse sports as a total, we have to break down the silos that everybody is in – I'm an eventer, I'm a natural horseman, I'm a hunter rider – if we are going to make some changes. The problem with that thinking is that we

'At the moment, the clients pay for it all, and if it stays that way, we hit the top of the bubble. Unless we get spectators involved, get outside money coming in, we have to pay for it ourselves, and people can only pay so much.'

don't think of ourselves as horsemen, in an equine industry. So show jumping tries to promote itself, and eventing tries to promote itself, and dressage tries to promote itself, but the numbers aren't big enough. Whereas if we promoted ourselves much more as a horse industry, our numbers would be huge and then we could tap into opportunities for television, sponsors and so on. This is why Karen and I go and do so many different things. We will go and sit in on a reining clinic, or a cutting show, or sit on a saddlebred. We have that opportunity, being the number one eventing couple, and so can break down the barriers.

'We have to do this if we are to survive as an industry. The problem is that at the moment, the clients pay for it all, and if it stays that way, we hit the top of the bubble. Unless we get spectators involved, get outside money coming in, we have to pay for it ourselves, and people can only pay so much.'

TINA: *David is an extraordinary person. He gives so much of himself, not just to his horses and his students, but to the sport as a whole. In recognition of this, in 2003 he was awarded the Wofford Cup, presented to people who have made outstanding contributions to the sport of eventing in a non-riding capacity. He was the first rider ever to receive this award.*

David holds a big vision, both for the training of horses and the future of the sport. He and Karen have already heralded so many changes in eventing, as much by their example of bravely going into new territories, as their outstanding competitive records. If he succeeds in spreading a common language between both human beings and horses, and between the horse sports themselves, he will have changed the direction of the equestrian world for ever. However, even extraordinary people have their off moments. As we end the interview, his helpers try to hang one of the barn doors. It sticks out at an angle: David has nailed the top fitting in too low. 'This has not made my night,' he says. It is time to retire with a Jack Daniels and a Diet Coke.

Rodrigo Pessoa:
Focus, Focus, Focus

Rodrigo Pessoa

Three times winner of the World Cup, and World Champion at the age of just twenty-five, Rodrigo is one of the most skilful and prolific winners in show jumping today. Son of the legendary Nelson Pessoa, his horses stand out for the thorough way in which they are prepared, and the fluid and enthusiastic way they jump, whilst as a rider he combines immaculate style with a fierce competitive instinct.

'The most important thing my father taught me was to be a good horseman, before being a good competitor. This is because the horse that is happy is going to deliver more than the horse that is not. He will try harder for you.'

Rodrigo Pessoa, like all international competitors, is a well travelled man; only last weekend he had won the World Cup qualifier in Geneva. He had been home for a day or so, before travelling to Olympia on the Thursday. When I spoke to him at 11.30 a.m. to fix up our meeting in London, he was still on the train from Brussels, although he was due to be jumping in a class at 1 p.m. The week was to continue in a similar vein. The next day he was placed second in the Christmas Cracker Stakes at Olympia; he then flew to Spain to La Corugna where he was placed in two classes on the Saturday, before returning to Olympia, London, on the Sunday for the World Cup qualifier. When I raised my eyebrows at this schedule, he just shrugged, and said, 'Well, if you want to stay at the top…'

It is easy to go into hyperbole when describing the way Rodrigo Pessoa rides: there is a grace and a unity with the horse that is hard to explain. At best one can point out his supreme body control and innate balance, combined with an elastic athleticism that absorbs the horse's movement, so it appears that the horse and he are working as one. This makes it easy for his horses to carry him, and they certainly tend to have a confident, enthusiastic expression, and a willingness to get on with the job.

To cap it all, his performances often look effortless. The only give-away of the focus that he puts into a round comes when he sometimes blows out his cheeks at the end of it, as if to say 'Wow, that took something!'

In short, some people are consummate horsemen, and others are excellent competitors who make up for shortcomings in technique by having a strong competitive spirit. Rodrigo has both. And in a more envious moment, it would seem that there is some magic he possesses that sets him apart from other riders. One could say it is in his genes. His father Nelson became one of the most outstanding show jumpers of all time, winning the Hamburg Derby seven times, and the Hickstead Derby three times. He was still competing at the highest level after more than thirty years, coming fifth at the World Games in The Hague in 1990, on Chouman, as well as having many victories on Vivaldi and Special Envoy in the late eighties and early nineties. With this history behind him, it is easy to think that Rodrigo was destined for success. But just like a well-bred young horse, genes are not enough to make him a success.

Early days

'We had the ponies in the back yard at home. The ponies were there, and I could ride if I wanted to, or not, but my father never really pushed me. At that age I did a lot of different sports: judo, swimming, tennis, soccer, and the ponies were there and I would ride once in a while, but in the beginning I was not that keen to ride. I was interested in other things, and I only really got hooked when I started competing. I thought the competition feeling was really great, so when I was thirteen or fourteen, that's when I got the virus of riding.'

> **TINA:** *This competitive spirit took hold quickly, because Rodrigo tasted success at an early age. He won his first Grand Prix in 1990, and was just nineteen when he rode in his first Olympic Games, coming ninth individually. At the next two Olympic Games he was the pivotal member of the bronze medal-winning show-jumping team. Most importantly, he won the World Championship in 1998, when he was twenty-five years old. In those early years, his father was a strong influence, and I wondered what his father might have taught him, that gave Rodrigo the edge over his fellow competitors.*

Getting the horse 100 per cent

'The most important thing he taught me was to be a good horseman, before being a good competitor. This is because the horse that is happy is going to deliver more than the horse that is not. This is the number one point: if he feels good, if he is sound and in a good state of mind, he will give a much better performance. He will try harder for you. So we have to look into having the horse in the best way possible, and I think this is the most difficult thing to do. The training, the jumping, the competition is not that hard afterwards.

'The most difficult thing is to get to know the horse well, find the little details and solve them, to get the horse 100 per cent. It's a permanent state of research with every horse.'

TINA: This 'permanent state of research' takes place at the Pessoa stable in Belgium. Although of Brazilian nationality, Rodrigo grew up in France, before the family moved to Belgium in the mid-eighties. The current Pessoa establishment is a beautiful complex, a huge indoor school surrounded by fifty indoor stables, of which Rodrigo has his own block of fifteen. The rest of the stables are taken up with Nelson's various students, including the Saudi Arabian show-jumping team.

Although Rodrigo comments that the training is not so difficult when you look after the horses' mental and physical well-being to the highest degree, it is still an integral part of producing great show jumpers. What strikes me when I watch Rodrigo warm up for a class, is the fluidity and softness with which his horses work, particularly through a turn or a circle. They maintain the same soft, consistent inside bend in walk, trot and canter. The famous Australian trainer Franz Mairinger said, if you can ride a corner correctly, you know it all, and this is certainly true of Rodrigo's horses.

The horse's ridability

'The horse must be also "disponsible" ["available" in French] to lengthen, to shorten, and to carry themselves in the most natural way possible. I don't like the horse to have his chin stuck to his chest. I have a lot of respect for the way the horse is built, and the way they like to go. For me, the one thing they have to be is light in the mouth. I am not strong, and I don't want to have to ride with strength. If they want to have their head in place, or straight up, it doesn't matter, but they must be light.

'After this, the horse must be in front of your leg. This is very important so you can lengthen the stride, but also so you can shorten the stride. If you are going to win, you always need to work on the horse's ridability. To do this, I work a lot on the flat and over small obstacles, in order to get him 100 per cent ridable.'

TINA: A typical Rodrigo training session looks like this:

A typical training session

'Normally I start by walking around a little. The horse will have done twenty minutes walking on the treadmill before, so he has had some warm-up. After doing some trot, I do small circles, lateral movements, then lengthening and shortening the trot, perhaps leg-yield each way. Everything you do to one side, you need to do on the other. Then in the canter, I do a lot of transitions, a lot of

> 'The horse must be also "disponible" ["available" in French] to lengthen, to shorten, and to carry themselves in the most natural way possible. I have a lot of respect for the way the horse is built, and the way they like to go.'

changes of direction and leg so the work does not become too monotone, too heavy. I let the horse play a little while he is working, to keep him happy.

'I might pop him over a little cavaletti or a Liverpool, maybe let the horse buck a little. If the horse enjoys his work, he will stay right in his head. I do work over poles on the ground and cavalletti, often making figures-of-eight over them, all the time to improve the horse's ridability. Maybe I will jump little fences, keeping the horse nice and soft, having him wait for the jump.

'Normal jumping we do maybe once a week, or once every two weeks. The jumpers, if they have it, they have it. They can always improve a little bit, but if a horse does not have the ability from day one, he is not going to be a good show jumper.'

TINA: *It is no coincidence that the best riders in the world also ride the best horses. Just as Pete Sampras would not use a wooden tennis racket, it is not worth a good rider sitting on an ordinary horse. But picking a good horse is an art in itself, so I asked Rodrigo what he looked for when he goes to try a horse.*

What to look for in a horse

'The first thing is to see how the horse looks, what his expression is, how he moves. His general attitude and ridability are very important. With a young horse, you have to try and imagine what the finished product will be, but that is a difficult thing to imagine, what he will be like with two or three years' work, in just fifteen or twenty minutes.

'I want him to be intelligent, so I look at his reactions to what I ask him, how he reacts to his environment, if he listens, if he corrects himself after a mistake. Also does *he* correct *himself*, or do I have to make the correction? These all make up his general attitude.

'It is also more important to me that the horse is careful, than how scopey he is. If a horse is careful, you can always find a category for him to go in. He will find his place in the stable. But if he is not so careful, but has all the scope, then it is not worth jumping him in so many classes, because he is always going to have four or eight faults. So when I look for a horse, of course I want one with all the scope and that is careful enough to win championships, or a horse that is careful and can jump intermediate level classes.'

> TINA: The icing on the cake of this attention to detail to all aspects of the horse's life and training is to perform well at a competition. But before you get in the ring, there is the last bit of preparation to handle, and it is an old maxim that competitions are won or lost in the warm-up.

The importance of the warm-up

'Sometimes I will work the horse a little on the flat in the morning before a class to loosen him up a bit. You need to do the best warm-up possible to give the horse the best chance of jumping a good round. That means you need to know your horse well, to know exactly what he needs: not too much, not too little.

'I look for the horse to show when he is ready to go. That is not so much what happens at the last warm-up fence, but a combination of all the fences you have jumped, and the feeling that builds up from that. Sometimes though, the horse warms up well but jumps badly in the ring; other times the horse does not feel so good in the warm-up, but can try hard in the ring.

'Baloubet is a horse who has bad concentration. He doesn't pay attention to what he is doing, until he touches a fence. If he makes a mistake it will be at the beginning of the round because he is not into it yet. So I try to have a little rub with him outside just before he goes in, so he focuses; but it's not always easy to do.'

> TINA: Of course, the horse is only one half of the partnership. To get the right result, at the right moment, the rider also has to have the right mental attitude. Rodrigo is a master at keeping his cool. In the first round of the Individual competition at the last Olympics, Baloubet de Rouet was unfocused and ran on a bit, kicking out the second fence and having the upright down after the water fence. At this point it would have been easy to have dismissed any chance of a medal. However, Rodrigo entered the arena for the second round as focused as ever, and coaxed a clear round from the still slightly

> 'I look for the horse to show when he is ready to go. That is not so much what happens at the last warm-up fence, but a combination of all the fences you have jumped, and the feeling that builds up from that.'

onward-bound Baloubet, over a course that was a match for most of the early leaders, resulting in a silver (that became gold) medal. But had Rodrigo always been this way?

A different approach

'I used to try too hard sometimes because I wanted to do too well, and so I missed a lot of good results, a second, or third or fourth perhaps, and ended up eighth or ninth because I tried too hard; but this was my character. Today, my approach is totally different. I concentrate on what is more important. The beginning of the week at a show is not that important, and I look to my bigger goals, and wait to be ready on a certain day. That is the point that has changed in me in the last couple of years. I don't go to win every class: rather, today's class was the preparation for something more important.'

TINA: It is this sort of range of vision that makes Rodrigo the consistent winner he is. As an example, in 2003 the mare Bianca d'Amaury competed in thirty-one classes, winning eight of them, and coming second another seven times. In all she was placed twenty-two times out of those thirty-one classes. Furthermore, he is a rider who consistently produces the right result at the right time, having won the World Cup three times, and being placed second in 2003.

There is no doubt that Rodrigo has a special talent for this type of production, but it is the overall attention to detail that makes him the winner, rather than just his competitive edge.

A professional sport

'We have entered a very technical era. The preparation of the horses and riders is much better, the horses work much better on the flat, and are more under the rider's control. This causes the course builders to scratch their heads much more, not to build courses that are crazily big, but to build more difficult, technical tracks to get the right number of clears. It has upgraded so much that it is an entirely professional sport now.'

> TINA: This technicality is reflected in courses having testing combinations of related distances. For example, in the second round of the Individual final in Athens, the most difficult line consisted of a very wide triple bar, followed by five short strides to a treble consisting of a vertical, one stride to another vertical and then a long stride to a huge parallel. It caught out a lot of riders and horses. It required the horses to have tremendous scope, but also to respond immediately to the rider's request to shorten, whilst keeping their attention on the treble ahead. If the rider over-dominated the horse, they lost impetus and could not make the distance in the treble. If the horse resisted the rider's requests to shorten, they ran themselves into the bottom of the first part of the treble.

The way forward?

'It is difficult to see where we can go further. You cannot go much faster in jump-offs or jump much higher than we do now. The skill is now to be ready on the right day. There are so many good horses and riders. Out of forty riders in a class, there are twenty-five riders who can easily win it. The competition is so tough.'

> TINA: All of this makes international show jumping a truly professional sport, and the riders who compete, professional athletes. With this is mind, Rodrigo feels a responsibility to promote the sport and encourage young riders, as well as being as good an ambassador for the sport as possible.

Show jumping's ambassador

'It's not enough just to win classes: you need to do things outside the ring, too. I am closely involved with the FEI and the rider's club, and in order to promote the sport we need to get better TV coverage so we can reach more people. This is a goal we have.'

'It is difficult to see where we can go further. You cannot go much faster or jump much higher than we do now. The skill is now to be ready on the right day.'

TINA: *To remain at the top of the sport, Rodrigo needs to be out competing constantly. Whereas when his father started his international career he attended one or two shows a month, Rodrigo competes at over forty shows a year, often four or five days long.*

And after competition...

'I have been competing for fifteen years at this level, and am starting to get a little tired. Right now I have some good owners and a great string of horses, so we will see after the next Olympic Games. After that I think I would like to spend more time with my family and do things I don't have time for right now. For the next four years, though, I will concentrate on my job, and will then review it afterwards.

'I will not be competing in thirty years time like my father was. I admire the tenacity and courage of the older riders like John and Michael who started twenty-five, thirty years ago, but I have other priorities – although for the moment my priority is my job. Nevertheless there are other things in life, apart from competition.

'I will still be involved with horses, maybe have a couple of horses with somebody, and from time to time I will come to a horse show and say hello to everybody. So I will be involved with horses, but without the obligation of being there every day.

'I am pretty keen to help young riders. I already have a twenty-year-old boy riding for me, and I push him a little – he is talented and has a good head, and I think he can become a good rider. The other thing I may do is help promote the sport, to work with sponsors to organize a show. Something that does not require the same amount of travelling, but it has a big impact on the sport.'

TINA: *Someone once told me that the art of enjoying a party is to know when it was time to leave. It seems that Rodrigo is applying his excellent focus that currently* serves him so well as a horseman and a competitor, to his life in general.

Rodrigo's strength comes from his simple clarity. He knows exactly how he wants things to be. Of course, simplicity does not always make something easy to do, but his patient adherence to what he believes in, the sound education of his horses, matched with his own innate talent, is what makes him almost unbeatable.

It is true that Rodrigo has had a golden opportunity since birth: born to one of the greatest horsemen of all time, and now with outstanding facilities, and owners who can buy him very good horses. But he is also a man who has made the very best of this opportunity, pouring his whole self into his sport.

One of my father's lasting memories of Nelson Pessoa was Nelson's maxim, that if you saw someone doing something well, you should practise it until you could do it better than them. This seems to be advice that Rodrigo absorbed early in life. It is not so much that he does anything different from his contemporaries, it is just that he does it better.

Mark Rashid and the Art of Passive Leadership

Mark Rashid

Although he comes from a Western background, Mark eschews complicated training methods and the label of 'natural horseman', instead saying he just tries to help horses and riders get along better. He travels around the world giving clinics, sharing his deep understanding of horse and human psychology and putting it into practice in the most simple of ways, bringing revelation to even the most novice of riders.

Spending several hours sitting in an indoor school on a grey January day, wrapped in every piece of winter clothing I can find, is not my idea of fun. However, I am here to see Mark Rashid work, a quietly spoken man, whose cowboy hat and chaps give away his roots. Based in Colorado, but travelling all over the States, and increasingly to Europe, he devotes his life to teaching gentle but effective methods of training horses. Of all my interviewees, he is the one I know the least about. Nevertheless, having read some of his books, and talked to friends who are involved in the natural horsemanship world, I am curious to see him in action. And after a few minutes, I am fascinated.

Mark bases his teaching on what he calls 'passive leadership'. Passive does not mean a limp, ineffectual type of approach: rather, it is a phrase that describes the way a certain type of horse, usually placed in about the middle of the hierarchy, attracts a lot of followers within the herd.

The most easily identifiable leader in the herd is the alpha horse. He is the one who gets to the food first, and chases others away until he has had his fill. He, or she, is the dominant animal, and threatens the other horses with a swift bite or kick if they step out of their place in the pecking order. In Mark's observance, this is also the attitude that many people come from, to a greater or lesser degree, when they train horses, and it can be very effective in getting the horse to do what you want.

But the passive leader, the horse that Mark models his work on, is the horse that leads by example, rather than force. They may not even particularly want to be a leader, but because the atmosphere around them is calm and content, other members of the herd are soon attracted to them. From Mark's observance, a horse's number one desire is to survive, to make sure he sees tomorrow, and all of his decisions are based on fulfilling that desire. Therefore, given the choice of either being constantly chased around, or being able to graze quietly, they will opt for the latter, because that way they conserve energy to use if some dangerous or threatening situation occurs.

expert insight

'The reality is that there are two emotions that control the horse from the day he is born to the day he dies, and they are on the opposite ends of the spectrum. One of them is curiosity, and the other one is fear.'

The passive leader is dependable and consistent in his behaviour, and Mark's approach is to demonstrate those qualities to the horses he is working with. This builds trust between him and the horse, and then he is in a position to start making requests of the horse.

Building trust

'I try not to stifle anything in the horse. The reality is that there are two emotions that control the horse from the day he is born to the day he dies, and they are on the opposite ends of the spectrum. One of them is curiosity, and the other one is fear. A fearful horse can't be curious, and a curious horse can't be fearful; so if you can turn fear into curiosity, you've got them, and if you can keep any curiosity that is there, the chance of them being fearful is a long way off.

> TINA: This was beautifully demonstrated by a foal that had been brought along to the clinic. The first day, Mark had worked on establishing boundaries, so the foal was easier to lead. The next day, he introduced him to a trailer.

A different perspective

'I try to use whatever the horse offers up, like with that baby I loaded in the trailer. You need to know that what he might offer up may not look like what you think it should look like, because he is coming at the situation from a different point of view, so I try to use that to my advantage, rather than working against it.'

> TINA: This is one of the early points that Mark makes in the clinic, that the response the horse gives you, when interpreted from the human being's point of view, can look like resistance.

Using what the horse offers up

'And that is just trial and error over the years, knowing that any horse you bring up to a trailer that is struggling, is going to pull, and if you pull hard enough, he is going to pull you out of that trailer. But rather than doing that, know that he is going to give you a little pull that says, "I am trying to come in". Now it doesn't look like it's supposed to look like, it's supposed to be coming forwards, but it's going to be backwards before it's forwards. So when you feel that little backward pull, you release, and then they come to you with a loop in the rope. So I think it's really important to use whatever the horse is offering up, in this case curiosity.'

TINA: *This is indeed what happened. The foal walked close to the ramp, stopped, gave a little snort and jerked his head back. It was as if he said 'I want to come with you, but I'm not sure.' By releasing the rope, Mark said 'I hear you'. When the release came, the foal stepped forward again, sniffed the ramp and jumped back. Mark released. When he felt the foal was ready, he lightly touched the rope. The foal stepped forward and put one foot on the ramp. Mark released immediately. He continued in this consistent fashion, and after about five minutes, the foal walked into the trailer. As soon as he had done that, Mark took him out of the trailer, and repeated the scenario.*

In this way, what Mark is teaching is not so much a technique, as an attitude. The This attitude is that the horse is basically trying to do what you want, and if you look at the situation from his point of view, you will be able to find a solution for whatever problem is occurring.

An important key to this work is Mark's appreciation of what he calls a 'try'. That is, whenever you ask the horse something, he will give a response of some kind, and as soon as that response comes, you must recognize and reward it. If you do not, the horse will offer another 'try', often the opposite to what he first offered.

Mark also constantly reminds riders and handlers to release at the first moment of 'try', not waiting till after the horse has completed the action. This is especially true when the horse is learning something new, and is perhaps not sure of what response you want. As soon as he offers something, Mark asks the rider to release the cue (his word for aids). The horse gets the message 'Yes, that was what I wanted.' He will then offer more, the next time you ask. However, if the rider does not notice that first tentative offer, and keeps the pressure on, the horse will assume that he has not done what you wanted, and he will try something else.

To notice these 'trys' though, takes a kind of micro-awareness from the rider, and to be this aware, the rider needs to be focused.

Ride consistently

'When you go out to ride for an hour, generally you are actually riding for about twenty minutes. The other forty is spent thinking about what you are having for dinner or what your boss said at the office. This means that human beings are inconsistent – but horses love consistency, so make your goal to ride consistently, no matter what the situation.'

TINA: *Another of Mark's keys to working with the horse in the simplest fashion possible is to take advantage of its natural mechanics. For example, one rider had an attractive six-year-old horse that went in a soft and obedient way, and when it came to canter, struck off beautifully to the right. However, it also struck off beautifully to right canter on the left rein! But instead of getting stronger with the horse, or reprimanding him for the incorrect strike-off, Mark asked the rider to identify when the horse was taking a slightly longer trot stride with its left foreleg than its right. At this point it is physically easier for the horse to strike off on the left lead, so asking him at this moment is more likely to result in a correct strike-off. And after a couple of attempts, it did.*

Working with Walter

'This goes back to my early days when I was working with Walter. For him, fighting with a horse was far out of the realm of possibility – which isn't to say he wouldn't say to a horse, "Don't run me over"; but by the same token, when he was training, there was very little push and shove and banging and whacking. I don't even remember seeing it, which doesn't mean it wasn't there, but I sure don't recall it.'

TINA: *'Walter' – also known in some of his books as the 'old man' – is the person who provided Mark with nearly all his early education, and without ever describing it as such, introduced the young Mark to 'passive leadership'. He was an old cowboy, into whose fields Mark ventured as a boy, gradually getting to know the horses, and who taught Mark in a similar fashion to the way that Mark himself teaches. On their first meeting – or rather, the first time Mark realized that someone had spotted him – he ran away as fast as he could, and didn't come back for months.*

Mark then worked out a strategy, checking the yard for the truck before going into the field. However, on one occasion he had become so engrossed in the horses that he did not notice anyone coming until a finger tapped him on the shoulder. He was simply asked the question 'Are you coming?' as the old man walked off. Given the space to either come or to leave, Mark's curiosity overtook him and he followed the old man back to the barn, where his education as a horseman would begin.

Training in Aikido

'Walter was the most important influence on me, because he was the first; and then there were my horses, particularly my old horse Buck. But it is all tied together by Aikido. Before I did Aikido, I had a lot of pieces floating around. I talk about having links in your chain of learning, and the longer your chain obviously the easier it is going to be for you to connect with new information. I thought I had a really long chain, and then I found I had a lot of links, but they weren't together. When I started training in Aikido, the pieces started to connect. There were links in my chain that I didn't know I had, and other links that I thought I had, but I didn't really. Aikido was the glue that put it all together... is putting it together. I'm not saying I'm there yet, and I may never be. But I can see now where the path has got clearer and wider, and I can see where I am going.'

TINA: *Aikido is a martial art that Mark has practised for many years, and which has had a direct influence over his training of horses and riders. This practice is self-evident by his stance. Throughout the day, Mark stood quietly and squarely over his feet. When he walked it was with a measured but definite rhythm, mirrored by the voice with which he answered the many questions put to him.*

Being ahead of the game

'In Aikido, the whole idea behind what we do is to get a hold of, or take the other person's centre. This means that your centre should always be intact, and when someone attacks you, just by the mere fact that they are attacking you, they are already out of their centre, and so you are ahead of the game. But their centre is generally going to be somewhere in their body, up or down, and the idea is to get a hold of them and bring them or their centre to yours. So you become the centre of the hurricane, and all the mess is outside of you.

'The centre is just your place of power. That's all it is, and a really easy way to find your place of power, your centre, is to pick up a wheelbarrow of manure. You can't push it with just your arms or legs: you have to use your whole body. The power or the push comes from here [he points to a spot about 2in below his navel]. The horse's centre of power is directly underneath where the rider sits, conveniently. What happens, though, is that we are thinking so much, our centre ends up in our forehead, or our head, whereas we need it down here, just below the navel.'

'My perspective, and it comes from my martial arts training, is to be able to do the same thing with the horse as we do in martial arts. That is, we take the centre of the person who is attacking you, and we turn it into a positive thing, instead of a negative thing.'

TINA: Mark demonstrated the power of this with a person standing on the floor. First he asked her to put all her attention on her forehead. He pushed her shoulder and she stepped back quite suddenly. Then he asked her to move her attention down to her chest area. Again, he gave her shoulder a gentle push, and she swung back, but not as dramatically. Then he asked her to put her attention to the spot below her navel. This time when he pushed her, she hardly moved.

The 'way of harmony'

'My perspective, and it comes from my martial arts training, is to be able to do the same thing with the horse as we do in martial arts. That is, we take the centre of the person who is attacking you, and we turn it into a positive thing, instead of a negative thing. Aikido translates into "the way of harmony", so even when someone is attacking you, the aim is to bring everything to a harmonious conclusion.'

TINA: In equestrian terms, this often means finding the solution that is staring you in the face. One horse that was brought to the clinic was lame and short-striding in front. The owner was desperately keen for the horse to go barefoot − that is, without shoes − but this horse had a history of laminitis and other foot problems, and was patently not happy with that, and Mark quietly suggested that the owner should have a pair of front shoes put on the horse. Mark is an advocate of horses going barefoot, but this horse was telling his rider, 'That does not suit me'. Likewise, a horse that swished his tail was not, Mark believed, disrespectful. He had brought a friend of his along who was a highly experienced chiropractor, who went to work on the horse. The horse was indeed very sore from the saddle that was pressing on his lumbar vertebrae.

> 'If you want to go truly natural, you need to take your horse's shoes off, put a hemp rope around his neck, get yourselves somewhere just south of Montana, take off all your clothes, and now ride your horse.'

A relationship with the horse

'It's about finding the simplest solution. Why are we making it so complicated? We're in a relationship, that's all this is, right?'

> **TINA:** In this way Mark is refreshingly lacking in dogma. He eschews the ideas of techniques, both in a rigid construct of how the horse should react in any given situation, or the need for extensive equipment, that sometimes comes as part of the natural horsemanship package. His only equipment appears to be a lunge line, a halter, and a huge dose of common sense. He prefers to work with whatever the rider and horse have, right here and now. Anyway, he comments with a twinkle in his eye, there is no such thing as natural horsemanship.

Going truly natural

'If you want to go truly natural, you need to take your horse's shoes off, put a hemp rope around his neck, get yourselves somewhere just south of Montana, take off all your clothes, and now ride your horse.'

> **TINA:** What becomes more and more clear throughout the day is that Mark is not so much working with the horses, as with the people. After all, the horse already knows how to be a horse. It is the human being who needs to learn how to be a horseman. To this end, Mark usually starts a session by asking a rider what they want to do.

Learning to be a horseman

'One of the things that a lot of the work that comes under the banner of natural horsemanship does is take the responsibility away from the rider. In my view, you are responsible for your own learning: you have to come in here with a plan, and if you don't have one, we will sit and wait here until you do. I can steer somebody in a direction, if a rider is nervous or worried, and with those people I will help them find their way. So that's the first step for me, to put some responsibility back on the rider, to make some decisions for their horse. So we start right there. "What do you want to do?"

"Well, I don't know, you're the trainer."

"Yes, but you're the one on that horse. I don't know the horse, and I don't know you, so you are going to have to come up with something here."'

TINA: In this situation, even if the rider has come with a request that is perhaps beyond them on this day, Mark can track back to a point that might need to be addressed in order for them to progress to their original desire. The bottom line is, at least the rider has made a decision, and that is the beginning of taking responsibility for their learning.

'And we might find a way to get them to that point. Or not, depending on what happens.'

TINA: Sometimes it can work in reverse. One rider had brought a charming chestnut horse along, who was also rather one-sided. Her wish was to work on getting the horse even on both reins, and this they did by working on a figure-of-eight. Then Mark introduced a simple change within the figure-of-eight, and it soon became obvious the horse was offering to make a flying change. The rider said 'I can't do that,' and Mark suggested they try anyway, and the horse made a flying change.

The ease with which the horses and riders made progress was partly facilitated by the way the riders sat. Mark talked about the riders carrying themselves inside a vertical belt, and in particular, how important it was to keep their heads inside that vertical belt. After all, when you see a calm, balanced person walking around, they rarely have their head stuck in front of them. That is the physical stance of a person who is in a rush. Therefore by helping the riders to be physically 'centred', they started to align mentally too, and this allowed them to be more sensitive to what was happening underneath them.

Similarly, he used the image of 'dumping the water out of the pelvic bowl'. This means that when the rider leans back, it rolls the pelvic bowl forwards and tips the water out. Imagining the water staying in the bowl helps the rider maintain their centre of gravity. He also did an exercise with the first rider, who was a little nervous, by asking her to identify which of her hips was moving when. As the left hip rose, the left hindleg was coming forward, as their leg went towards the horse's barrel, the front leg was coming forward. When the rider becomes more aware in this way, they become more sensitive to the little 'trys' the horse might offer them.

I asked Mark if he had worked on the seat specifically the day before.

Working on the rider

'Most of the riders sat pretty well so we did not do a lot. I talked about breathing and moving with the horse to everybody to some degree, and then Kathleen (his assistant) worked on some of that as well.

'But a lot of times I'll leave the rider alone, because if we start there, it's like I'm saying, "Okay we need to fix you before we can do anything with the horse." What I really want to have is the rider say "Boy, do I need to work on this."

'So I might touch on it, throw a little shot over the bows, say something like, "You're not moving as well with that horse as you could." Then I leave it, and have them come back a little later and say "What do you mean by that?" and I'll reply "Oh, it's just this…Don't worry about it" and throw that in, too. "If you need to think about it, think about it, but don't worry about it." This gives them permission to get that, rather than thinking, "Gosh, that's what I really have to work on," and the rest of it goes out the window.

'I don't make a big deal out of it, just let them put it to the back of their mind for a couple of days, and then give it some thought. That gives them permission to open up a little more, and think about it while they are doing something else. I've found that's pretty beneficial.

'Of course, if the seat is blatantly bad and it's causing all the issues, we will start working on it right there and then. But if we can get around it and we can deal with the most important thing first, say if the horse is throwing his head right back in the rider's face, then we are going to have to take a look at that first, because never mind how they are riding, that is dangerous.'

expert insight

'Don't make unimportant things important. Horsemanship is for life: it's not about changing your horse, but changing your life, too. Do your work away from the horses, and then bring it to him.'

TINA: The results of Mark's work are quite tangible. One horse started a session neighing his head off, and as a result the rider was quite nervous of it. Mark worked with the rider in a quiet, logical way, setting the horse and rider small tasks. Given something specific to do, the horse settled down and began to concentrate on his work. Another horse that was resisting going in a soft shape, become rounder and softer as the session went on, and ceased fighting the rider. Naturally, this happened around about the time that the rider stopped fighting the horse. Even more surprisingly for me, although Mark has strong Western influences in his upbringing, all the horses went in a conventional round shape; indeed if you popped your head over the door momentarily, you could have been mistaken for assuming this was a traditional dressage lesson going on.

Now this is a common scenario with almost any experienced horseman. The difference was that this was all done with no fuss. I never heard Mark raise his voice, or even his tone change much. This can only be attributed to the work he has done on himself, especially through Aikido. As he said himself, Aikido is so important to him that he shapes his diary around his classes, not the other way around. Also, the riders did not have to work physically very hard, although they may have become tired from the mental concentration.

Horsemanship is for life

'If you live your life in a panic, then when your horse spooks, you will spook. Don't make unimportant things important. Horsemanship is for life: it's not about changing your horse, but changing your life, too. Do your work away from the horses, and then bring it to him.'

TINA: I was so inspired by watching Mark. I thought about human leaders who push their weight around a lot, and how uncomfortable it is being around them. For a moment I fantasized about a world where everyone led by example, and so I asked Mark, if the passive leader is so successful, how come there are still alpha horses in the herd?

The herd hierarchy

That's the hierarchy of the herd. It has to happen that way. The older stallions that fight for their territory, eventually they are going to get kicked out. But the older mares will stay, and may or may not chase the others around. But in order for the herd to function properly — and this is just my idea, I don't have anything to prove it – there is a lot of turmoil within the herd, and it appears that the alpha has to be there to keep order, but the other horses don't like it much and so they need a quiet place to go to, where they can still be led but they don't have to worry about getting kicked or bitten. It's the structure of the herd, and it has worked really well for fifty million years, so we're not going to re-invent the wheel here.

'This is just what I've observed amongst wild horses, and amongst big herds of domestic horses, where there aren't any stallions. So I think it's just the way it's supposed to work. That passive leader is a safe place the horses can go, a port in a storm. Plus they get to follow, and most horses are born followers.'

> TINA: The root of Mark's work is a great deal of acceptance of what is in front of him. He aims to see it as truthfully as he can, coming from a compassionate, though not weak, standpoint, and that standpoint is not 'This horse has a problem', but 'How can I relate what I want in a way this horse can understand?'

Working with the horse

'It doesn't have to be that hard. If someone has used a lot of pressure, what's our alternative? Use less pressure, but use it differently, so you work with the horse, not against it. I'm not interested in fighting with the horse. It's too much hard work.'

> TINA: The measure of a person is how much they 'walk' their talk. Mark does not force his ways on horses, nor does he force his methods on people. He simply demonstrates an attitude that has worked for him, and leaves the audience to make the choice for themselves. What he showed me was, if you create an attitude inside yourself that works with the horse, you not only remove the possibility of a lot of the problems you might encounter in your training, but you also create the situation from which you can solve any that might come along. And that is the best lesson anyone could learn.

Afterword

So did I succeed in my mission to find the essential core of each person's success?

Yes, I think I probably did. Each of the interviews has a different flavour, and some will have appealed to you more than others. But when you look closely, you will realize that they actually share a common core. More than that, it is not a technique, but an attitude that is at the heart of their work. It is that, above all, they are horsemen and women. They have studied, with great love and great care, the art of horsemanship. They have discovered how a horse mentally and physically functions, and worked with that knowledge. They have, if you like, taken a walk in their horse's shoes.

By doing this they have created relationships based on trust and mutual understanding. These kinds of relationships, developed over time, have produced the results the trainers wanted, whether that is in the realm of competition, or just enjoying their day-to-day work.

The same can be true for you. I hope you enjoy the journey.

Index

aids 56–7, 61–2, 82, 92–4, 106–7, 126
Aikido 128–9
Alderbrook 11
automatic release 83

balance 93–5, 128–9, 131–2
Balkenhol, Klaus 40
Baloubet de Rouet 118–19
Battleship 68
Best Mate 65, 66, 68, 70, 74–6
Bianca d'Amaury 119
Biddlecombe, Terry 69–70, 75
bit, using 94–5, 102
body awareness 85–6
Boomerang 30
Border Raider 109
breathing 56–7, 132
Breisner, Goran 'Yogi' 9–24
Bunn, Dougie 30
buying and selling 26–8, 32–3, 50–1, 66–8, 69–70, 117–18

Calvarro 37
carriage 61–2
Cash, Ned 29
Cevera, Luis Alvarez 110
Channon, Mick 72
Charles, Peter 25–38
Chouman 115
Clark, Jane 54
Clawson, Kenneth 14
communication 18, 46–7, 93, 103
confidence 18, 19–20, 36, 87–8
confrontational training methods 45, 125–6
confusion, causing 82
consistency, importance 126–7
core problem, identifying 20–1, 130–1

Davenport, Richard 37
Davison, Richard 39–52
Deep Run 67–8
Dover, Robert 53–64
dressage 39–64, 91–100

Ehning, Marcus 37
Eros 90
ET 30
eventing 9, 11, 101–12

feeling, learning by 96
focus, maintaining 48–9, 81–2, 86–7
Forster, Captain Tim 68
forward riding, encouraging 23
Fox, Andy 72

Fox-Pitt, William 12, 14–15, 19
Funnell, Pippa 12–13, 15

Gandolpho, David 72
Giltedge 107
Grannusch 30
Grunsven, Anky van 48

half-halt 56–7
happy athlete' 45–6, 61
herd hierarchy 124, 133–4
Hobbs, Reg 68

jumping 44, 78–90, 97–8, 107–8

Kellet, Iris 29
Kennedy 54, 58–61
Klimke, Reiner 55, 80
Knight, Henrietta 65–76
Kottas, Arthur 40
Kursinski, Anne 77–90
Kyrklund, Kyra 91–100

le Goff, Jack 103, 105
limitations, respecting 99–100
loading 125–6
Lundqvist, Colonel 54, 64

Macken, Eddie 29–30, 35
Mairinger, Franz 116
Majiore, Lago 55
Master Oats 11
Matador 92
mental make-up of horse 95, 108–9, 125
Millman, Dan 81
Milton 30, 37
mistakes, making use of 16
Mon Santa 30
Morris, George 80–1

natural horsemanship 105–6, 110, 123–34
nerves, overcoming 17, 19, 36
Nieberg, Lars 37
Nordin, Sören 20

O'Connor, David 101–12
O'Connor, Karen 102, 103, 104, 112
Orlando, Holly 84
Osborne, Jamie 19
Otto 37

passive leadership 123–34
Pavitt, Louise 31
Pessoa, Nelson 113, 116, 121, 122

Pessoa, Rodrigo 37, 113–22
Pipe, Martin 72
pressure, dealing with 17

racehorses 65–76
Rashid, Mark 123–34
Ratina 30
Rehbein, Herbert 55, 96
Rembrandt 47–8
responsibility of trainer 46, 130–1
Robinson, Traci 15

Schultheiss, Willi 55
Schumacher, Conrad 40
seat 58, 83–5, 93, 96, 131–2
Sederholm, Lars 10–11, 66, 104–5, 109
self-awareness 12, 81–2
self-determination 34
Shannon 107
show jumping 25–38, 113–22
simplicity 18, 77–90, 127
Skelton, Nick 15, 37
Special Envoy 115
sports psychology 49
Sportsman 30
Stark, Ian 13
steeplechasing 65–76
Steinkraus, Bill 106
suppling 43–4

Tamarillo 14–15
telepathy 87–8
Tellington Jones, Linda 88
Theoderescu, Georg 55, 80
Tigre 30
Top Ville 68
trust, building 44–5, 125
Two Step 30

Ultimus 11
Un Desperado 68
Uphoff, Nicole 47–8

Vivaldi 115
Voorn, Albert 14

Walter 127–8
Welch, Sue and Fred 30
Werth, Isabell 48
Western halter 102–3
Western horsemanship 105, 110, 127, 133
Whitaker, John 48, 121
Whitaker, Michael 33, 48, 121
Williams, Cecil 30
Williams, Jimmy 78–80, 81, 85
Wilton Fair 104